INTERPERSONAL COMMUNICATION AT WORK

How to communicate with customers, bosses, colleagues, and subordinates

ROBERTA CAVA

Published by Cava Consulting

info@dealingwithdifficultpeople.info

www.dealingwithdifficultpeople.info

Cava, Roberta

Interpersonal Communication at Work

How to communicate with customers, bosses, colleagues, and subordinates

National Library of Australia

Cataloguing-in-publication data:

ISBN 978-0-6484437-6-6

BOOKS BY ROBERTA CAVA

Non-Fiction

Dealing with Difficult People (23 publishers – in 17 languages)
Dealing with Difficult Situations – at Work and at Home
Dealing with Difficult Spouses and Children
Dealing with Difficult Relatives and In-Laws
Dealing with Domestic Violence and Child Abuse
Dealing with School Bullying
Dealing with Workplace Bullying
Retirement Village Bullies
Keeping Our Children Safe
Just say no
What am I going to do with the rest of my life?
Interpersonal Communication at Work
Before tying the knot – Questions couples Must ask each other
Before they marry!
How Women can advance in business
Survival Skills for Supervisors and Managers
Human Resources at its Best!
Human Resources Policies and Procedures - Australia
Employee Handbook
Easy Come – Hard to go – The Art of Hiring, Disciplining and
Firing Employees
Time and Stress – Today's silent killers
Take Command of your Future – Make things Happen
Belly Laughs for All! – Volumes 1 to 6
Wisdom of the World! The happy, sad and wise things in life!

Fiction

That Something Special
Something Missing
Trilogy: Life Gets Complicated
Life Goes On
Life Gets Better

ACKNOWLEDGEMENT

My gratitude is extended to the thousands of participants of my seminars who have contributed ideas on how *they* handled their communication difficulties.

INTERPERSONAL COMMUNICATION

Being constructive
How to give and receive criticism
Who's perfect?
Accepting compliments

What kind of person are you?
Personality types
How to work with other personality types
Introvert and extrovert personality types
Approaches to conflict resolution
6 Styles of behaviour and their effects
Passive/aggressive/assertive people feel about themselves
Assertiveness blocks
Consequences of these behaviour styles

Paraphrasing
Using paraphrasing in training others
Sensory language
Different interpretation of words
Male and female interpretations
Feedback
Process of feedback
Feedback steps
Using feedback with very difficult people
Listening
Kinds of bad listeners
Blocks to effective listening
How do you rate as a listener?
Qualities of a good listener
Speaking
How do you rate as a speaker?
Avoiding ambiguous messages
Understanding non-verbal signals
Space bubbles
Eye contact
Arguments
Ways to reduce communication problems
Communication tips

No opportunity to acquire new skills
Absence of adequate job descriptions and
performance appraisals
Discrepancy between pay and level of responsibility
Unpaid overtime
The aggressive supervisor
Sarcasm
Ignoring or the *"silent treatment"*
Tantrums
Sexual harassment
Workplace Bullying

Poor delegation
Perfectionist
Poor disciplinary skills
Wants us to compete
Won't defend me
Does not give me credit for my contribution
Interferes with my supervision
Is unavailable to staff and clients
Does not respect privacy
Does not provide opportunities for advancement
Check your own attitude
Dealing with criticism

Unprofessional behaviour
Shirkers
Buck-passers
Putter-offers
Aggressive behaviour
Over-achievers and competitive types
Critical types
Interrupters
Personality conflicts
Conducting effective meetings
Dealing with problem participants at meetings

INTRODUCTION

When we speak of interpersonal skills - what do we mean? What skills does this involve?

- Speaking;
- Listening;
- Writing;
- Reading;
- Non-verbal communication (body language);
- Sensory language
- Understanding others (empathy); and
- Reacting to the behaviour of others.

Do you have problems communicating with others? It might be that your personality gets in the way or you simply do not feel comfortable communicating with others. You may prefer to communicate in writing – sending emails, texts or letters. Others may prefer to only communicate verbally. But we all need to communicate and try to understand where others are coming from in order to interact with others. We need to control our stress level, so it doesn't result in us blowing up at those who don't deserve it. Learning how to deal with the everyday stresses of life is one of the essentials to end up with good communication with others.

Reading this book should enable you to control your moods by not allowing others to give you a bad day. You'll learn how to control your anger and stress levels and obtain a psychological edge by improving your interpersonal skills.

Businesses (especially those offering services) are learning the importance of having employees who can handle all types of difficult people and situations and be able to express their company's vision to them. Employees who succeed in this area are in great demand.

You'll experience a feeling of accomplishment when you handle difficult situations well. You employer, co-workers and staff will trust and rely on you, will admire and like you, will think twice before pushing you around and will be more willing to try to please you.

If you're often misunderstood or others constantly misinterpret what you say or write, there are several skills that can correct these problems:

How do I know that the techniques outlined in this book really work? Because thousands of participants have attended my seminars and have given their input. Many took the time to write to me with examples of how they dealt with particularly difficult communication problems. These contributions are scattered throughout the book. I endorse every technique described here and use them regularly. Not only do I handle difficult situations better, but also, I've gained control of my reactions to negative situations. So can you!

CHAPTER ONE
UNDERSTANDING BEHAVIOUR
AND ITS EFFECTS

Do your moods control you?

Do you have mood swings that affect what kind of day you have? Are you up one day, down the next; up one hour, down the next? Many times, this depends on what's happening around you - somebody snarls at you or gives you a mountainous job to do. You think, *"Oh God, give me strength!"* It's the little annoyances that can ruin your day, so if you can handle them constructively, you're certainly ahead of the game.

Before you can tackle difficult people, it's essential that you have your own act together. Think of the last time you didn't feel in control during a trying situation. What happened to your self-esteem level? Most people find that their feeling of self-worth plummets after these kinds of encounters, so staying in control during difficult situations is essential for good mental health.

One way that can help you identify these kinds of situations is to be aware of the physical reactions happening to your body. The *"fight-or-flight"* syndrome kicks in whenever we encounter a difficult situation. Physical signs may include:

- tense muscles;
- gritted teeth or a clenched jaw;
- rapid pulse;
- a pounding heart;
- increased perspiration;
- shortness of breath;
- a rise in blood pressure;
- clammy skin;
- cold hands and feet; and
- rapid breathing.

Whenever you identify these signs in yourself, stop for a second and ask yourself: *"Am I reacting correctly, or am I overreacting to this situation?"* You'll find in about eight out of ten situations you've overreacted - given someone else control over the situation.

Too often, we let others control how we feel about ourselves. We allow them to give us bad days. We can attempt to change others' behaviour, but that might not happen. However, we do have control over how we react to their behaviour. My life changed when I realised that I could choose how I reacted when confronted with difficult situations. I could either take the bad feelings being handed to me by others or simply not take them. When I learned this simple technique, I found I had far more control over my everyday moods. Gone were the roller-coaster mood swings of the past. Other people didn't decide what kind of day I'd have - I did! You, too, can have this control. Mind you, there will be exceptions to this, but many moods and reactions you *can* control. If you control the little difficulties, you're better equipped to handle the big ones.

Angry Feelings

Picture this scene: You're driving to work, feeling pretty good about yourself and life. Suddenly, a car swerves in front of you, nearly causing a collision. You slam on the brakes (everything on the front seat goes flying) and hope for the best. Your car stops centimetres from the offending car. You peel yourself off the steering wheel, scrunch over to pick things up off the floor and look for the car that cut you off. It has disappeared.

What's your first reaction - to rant and rave about rotten drivers? How long do you stay mad at the driver of the other car? And what good does it do? I've seen people stay at fever pitch for hours, relating their experience to anyone who will listen.

When the car cut you off, you had two choices: you could stay upset about it, or admit you were in an emergency that you handled well and continue calmly driving to work.

If you *chose* to remain upset, you can't blame the other driver for it. What you do after something negative happens to you is *your* decision, not the other person's. If you allow someone else to upset you, you've made the wrong choice.

Dealing with Anger

Answer the following questions with:

1 = yes
2 = no
3 = sometimes

_____1. Do I usually walk away from the other person when I'm angry?

_____2. Do I usually keep quiet when I'm angry? (silent treatment?)

_____3. Do I simmer for days, then vent my anger on a big blowup?

_____4. Do I appear to feel hurt when I'm actually angry?

_____5. Do I take out my anger on someone other than the person at whom I'm angry?

_____6. Do I express my anger by labelling the other person rather than dealing with their behaviour?

_____7. When someone else is angry with me, do I have problems keeping my composure without blustering?

_____8. Do I have trouble "Keeping My Cool" when accused of something I didn't do and retaliate verbally?

_____9. Do I feel hurt and withdraw when someone is angry with me rather than facing the issue openly with that person?

Rating:

Answers 1 = yes: *You must work on*

Answers 2 = no: *No problems here*

Answers 3 = sometimes: *Judge for yourself whether these are causing you problems. If so, work on solving them.*

Check or circle the most applicable suggestion:

Dealing with my own anger

1. When I'm angry, I usually feel:

   a) Afraid to say anything directly, because I don't want to hurt others' feelings.

   b) Afraid that if I do say something, it will sound aggressive and others won't like me.

   c) Okay about expressing what is on my mind.

   d) Anxious and confused about what I want to say.

2. When I'm angry with someone, I usually:

   a) Drop hints about my feelings, hoping s/he will get the message.

   b) Tell the person in a direct way, what I want, and feel okay about it.

   c) Avoid the person for a while, while I calm down and the anger wears off.

   d) Blow up and tell him/her off.

   e) Express my anger sarcastically - getting my point across with some humour or a dig.

Dealing with Others' Anger

3. When someone gets angry with me, I usually:

   a) Think s/he doesn't like me.

   b) Feel too scared to ask why.

   c) Feel confused and upset.

   d) Think I have a right to understand why s/he is angry, and to respond to it.

   e) Immediately feel wronged.

   f) Feel guilty.

4. When someone gets angry with me, what I usually do is:

   a) End up blustering.

   b) Back off.

c) Ask him/her to explain his/her anger further, or else I respond to it in some other equally straightforward manner.

d) Get angry in return.

e) Apologize if I don't understand why s/he is angry.

f) Try to smooth it over.

g) Make a joke out of it and try to get him/her to forget the flare-up.

Rate Yourself:

The following answers indicate assertive beliefs and behaviours:

1. c)   2. b)   3. d)   4. c)

Repression of anger

Since childhood, men and women have been trained to hold back and control their negative feelings. This kind of conditioning results in two types of people:

Type A:

For whatever reasons, they have never learned to express their anger. No matter what the provocation, they clench their teeth and hold in their resentment. In some cases, they aren't even aware they're angry.

Type B:

They too haven't learned to appropriately express anger. Instead of ever showing displeasure over the minor, irritating day-to-day episodes that take place in everyone's life, they say nothing at the time. Then, a co-worker, salesperson, or friend makes a chance remark that triggers a red flash of rage, and on an unpremeditated basis, they lash out in violent anger. This fury has unfortunate consequences. The person feels terrible and they alienate others.

Both are extremes. Correct ways of dealing with anger means knowing your rights, appropriately expressing your feelings when someone tries to interfere with your rights, places an obstacle in your path, or violates your dignity. Uncontrolled lashing out, is not a positive expression of anger. Instead, after taking everything into consideration, you decide how best to express your anger. We're taught - incorrectly - that anger is a dangerous, powerful emotion. We believe that if we really get angry, we will lose somebody's love, provoke anger at ourselves in return, or that people won't like us. In fact, we've got it backwards. It is the repression of anger, not its expression, that is dangerous. Besides it doesn't matter a bit whether everyone likes you. That's an impossible goal, one that is guaranteed to frustrate you. People won't like you if you never get mad, in fact, they may like you less for it.

Depression: This can be anger that you turn against yourself because you feel so helpless about the situation. The resulting depression can become so severe that you think of suicide, even carry out the thought.

Displacement: Unable to face what you're really angry about, you shift it to another cause. For example something goes wrong at a party. You say nothing, but later blame your spouse for something s/he didn't do.

Long Fights: These often don't concern what you're angry about. They occur because you've shifted your goal from sharing to feelings of one of hurting the other person. You forget where you want to go. Your anger takes over and you can't stop yourself.

Temper Tantrums: This is inappropriate, uncontrolled expression of anger which can be set off by anything, whether some trivial current happening or something that took place long ago and which you've stewed about for years. We will be discussing this later.

Psychosomatic Illnesses: Your repression of anger can cause tension, insomnia, ulcers.

Anger is a very real part of everyone. The time has come for us to learn about anger, accept the fact that we have a right to it, and learn how to express it.

How to Handle Anger

1. Don't rationalize your reasons for not expressing anger.

Don't pay attention to such things as, *"I'm afraid to say anything because I'll hurt the other person's feelsings"* These are ways of explaining to yourself why you <u>don't do</u> what you've never learned to do. Instead of dwelling on the reasons why you don't express anger, concentrate on learning how to do it.

2. **Attempt to correct the behaviur of the person causing the anger – never attack the person themselves**

For example - a child spills his milk. Scold the child for the behaviour, don't attack him as a person. Say, *"Johnny, I'm upset. You spilled your milk again. Will you try to be morecareful next time?"* Instead of *"Johnny - you're so sloppy. Can't you be more careful?"*

3. **Target your angry behaviour. Get the pattern of your anger.**

a) The way you express anger:

- Do you show too little?

- Do you come on too strong, too weak, or not at all?

- Do you express anger days, months, even years after the provoking incident?

- Is your nonverbal communication of anger appropriate?

- Do you fall into the trap of attributing your anger to someone else? *("<u>You</u> make me angry!")*

- Do you mouth angry words, but say them in a whisper that the other person can barely hear?

- Do you slouch or keep your eyes on the floor as you say them?

Remember, you "own" your own responses. When you express anger, you should try to relate your comments to what the other person has done: *"I'm angry because you always leave the newspaper on the floor."*

b) The different situations in which you have difficulty.

- Is it at work? If so, break it down. Does your anger have to do with co-workers, subordinates, superiors?

- In impersonal situations? Some people allow themselves to get angry with taxi drivers or waitresses, and others that can never express annoyance back to them.

- Friends and acquaintances? With some people, the more distant the acquaintance is, the easier they find it to express anger. With others it's the reverse. The closer the friend, the easier it is to say, *"I'm furious."* There are some people who feel that the only time they're "being honest" is when they express anger.

- Social situations? Can you get angry in a group conversation, but not one-to-one?

- Do you feel safer in a group - or the reverse?

- In close relationships? Some can express anger only to a spouse. When asked *"Why?"* the answer is often, *"S/he is the only one in the world who wouldn't leave me if I show anger."*

- What time of the day do you become angry more often? What day of the week, or season of the year?

4. Recognize that you have a right to feel anger and to express it.

Anger doesn't have to lead to violence. If you have doubts about your right to be angry, perhaps you've done something you don't like, (feel you'd like to yell at yourself, and instead take it out on another person).

5. Express your anger when you feel it.

In this way, you can frequently avoid unpleasant consequences. Often you will lash out at the wrong person, for the wrong reasons.

6. Avoid direct expression of anger.

Perhaps you sit and sulk, seething inside, but refuse to say why you're angry. Or you communicate hurt instead of anger *("You souldn't have done this to me!")* Or you use sarcasm to express your anger, making it difficult for the other person to cope with the situation. They know something is wrong, but the sarcasm pushes them away and they can't pin down just what is bothering you. Be clear in your communication with them.

7. Don't make the mistake of not going far enough in your anger.

Some people make tentative stabs at expression of anger - then abort it. Don't just bring up the fact that you're angry - find a solution to the problem or situation that caused the anger in the first place.

8. Realize that you have the right to raise your voice.

It's perfectly all right to pound the table, swear, shout and do all the things "Mother" told you not to do - as long as you're not intimidating or taking advantage of another. Expressing anger doesn't involve just a higher voice level, it's the words you use, body position and movement. Some treat anger with silence or place distance emotionally between themselves and the other that has caused the anger.

9. Practice your new skills in a safe environment by:

- Role Play the situation with someone you trust.

- Monitor yourself - your level of anger on a scale of 1 - 10.

- Determine ways you could have handled your anger better than you did at the actual time of the anger.

- If there's someone to whom you feel close, but with whom you have trouble venting anger, write down all the things from the past that have made you furious with this person. Ask him/her to do the same. Then make an appointment to get together and discuss your respective lists.

- If your anger brings about tension and begins to interfere with other things you do, get it out of your system with physical exercise. This works when you're not in a position to express anger - for instance, the other person is out of the country.

- In your bedroom, hit your pillow for two minutes, curse into the pillow - release that anger.

- Grab your racquet ball racquet, write the face of the person you're mad at on the ball, and smash it into the wall (competitive sports at this time will only increase your stress level - not reduce it).

10. Make the deliberate decision not to express anger.

Initially, expressing anger may make you feel important. There are times, though, when you cannot express your anger. For example, with a frail older person who has stimulated anger in you. They may not be able to tolerate your anger health-wise.

11. Remember, your choice is not limited to expressing anger or not expressing it.

Sometimes you can use a supportive approach. For example - your boss yells at you and commands you to do something you consider completely unprofessional. Count to ten, then say *"Is theresomething wrong Mr............? I know there must be, or you would never speak to me that way."*

Common ways we see anger expressed at work

Direct - "take that!"

Usually our first response to a blocking condition is to directly attack it. Often this leads to very productive and creative effort. New procedures can develop this way. "Necessity is the mother of invention" - so some frustration can be desirable. However, if the blocking condition does not yield, we're likely to see direct expression of hostility which is destructive in intent - or we may see some of the less direct methods.

Example: A supervisor fails to recognize an employee's ability to come up with new ideas. The employee quits giving new ideas. The employee knows how s/he can do a faster, better job and feels frustrated that s/he can't try his/her own way. These employees will become "middle of the road" employees who appear to have tunnel-vision.

Sabotage - "lets get back at them!"

Sabotage in the work setting usually takes a much milder form than we typically associate with this word. Yet subtle forms of sabotage are very common. The work slow-down, the omitted procedure, the small "error," are all evidence of the frustration-anger model at work.

Example: A secretary who has to take notes at meetings but doesn't feels it's not her responsibility, so does a poor job of taking the minutes.

Over-compliance - "If that's what you want..."

One excellent way of expressing anger at the blocking boss, is to do exactly what s/he asks regardless of the circumstances. This practice can't be faulted by the boss, because after all, it's what s/he said, but s/he didn't mean to be taken so literally. Often when a union wants to make life difficult for management, the union starts going by the letter, rather than the spirit of the contract.

Example: You've given an employee a set of instructions on how to complete a project assuming s/he'll use his/her common sense and add pertinent information as necessary to complete the assignment. S/he didn't. The report is useless.

Emotional withdrawal - *"You aren't that important"*

One way to deal with continuing frustration, is to deny the importance of the blocking conditions. This is the familiar "sour grapes" attitude. We often see employees become apathetic and just "go through the motions" on the job - by their actions saying - this job isn't that important - the really important things for me are outside the job. If the interest and energy many workers spend on becoming star bowlers could be re-directed to the job - productivity gains would be considerable.

Example: An employee follows her job description to a *"T."* You, as her supervisor, know she's capable of much more.

Turning inward - *"It must be me"*

One of the most pathetic results of prolonged frustration, is the tendency on the part of some to turn their anger inward upon themselves. Instead of venting their anger against the blocking conditions through direct or indirect means, such as already listed, the individual begins to attack him or herself and winds up with a feeling of "actually I'm no good." Turning such a person around is a supervisory challenge of major magnitude.

Example: An employee who has taken a risk and has been "burned" - may retreat into themselves and refuse to make decisions - use tunnel-vision in completing assignments - must feel safe in any decision they make.

Dealing with hurt feelings

How do you react when a close friend or colleague says something that hurts your feelings? Do you withdraw into yourself and mull over the situation for a couple of weeks before you deal with it? Possibly the only thing that breaks the ice between you and that person is that s/he notices your reaction and say, *"What's wrong? You're so quiet."* You may or may not honestly explain about the comment that hurt your feelings. Instead of spending this time in misery, learn to:

1. Immediately identify that you're hurt;

2. Right away, talk with the person who gave you the bad feeling.

Depending on your personality, your response may range from, *"That last comment was below the belt. Can you tell me why you made such a comment?"* Or, *"That comment hurt my feelings - did you mean it the way I heard it?"*

Revenge

Someone has done something awful to you, and you don't care how long it takes you, but you're going to pay him or her back! You know what this is - *revenge.*

It feels good when we can pay someone back for a misdeed, but if you can't do so within a reasonable amount of time, let it go. If you analyse this situation, you'll realise that the other person has control over your life the entire time you're planning your revenge. In the meantime, you can't get on with your life and do constructive things. I've witnessed divorced people still planning revenge ten years after their divorce. What a waste of energy! I've also discovered that if you let it go and observe, you'll find that *"What comes around goes around"*, and the person is paid back for their misdeed without you having to waste your valuable energy.

If Only... I Should Have...

Do you spend your time wailing, *"If only I'd..."* or *"I should have...?"* What a waste of your life! Instead, concentrate on the present and the future - not the past.

Guilt

We live in a guilt-ridden society. Others take glee in pointing out our faults. My philosophy is that if you've done your best, that's all you can expect of yourself. If you didn't succeed at something, you haven't failed - you've learned something.

Do you feel guilty if you've made a mistake? Did you give your best effort? If so, the best way of dealing with your own mistakes (especially if someone else points them out) is to say, *"You're right – I did make a mistake. It won't happen again."* So, don't feel guilty if you've made a mistake. Instead, learn from it and don't do it again.

Here's another example. You've worked very hard completing an assignment and you're proud of your accomplishment. You wait... and *wait* for recognition from your supervisor. Is it likely to come? In many instances - no. You're more likely to hear about the small portion of the assignment you did wrong.

In addition to this, you're probably your own worst critic. We all have a little twerp in us all who is forever criticising us. It says such things as, *"You goofed again! Can't you do anything right?"*

Learn to stop criticising yourself and start giving yourself positive reinforcement. If you've done a good job, mentally pat yourself on the back with such thoughts as, *"I'm really proud of how I did that job."* Don't count on others to do this. If they do, think of their praise as *"gravy"* – but you don't need gravy on the potatoes every night, do you? Too much praise can make you swollen-headed. The person you should be trying to please the most is yourself. Never compete against the record of someone else. Just improve your own record of accomplishments.

The next time something like this happens to you, don't accept the negative feelings it causes. This takes hard, concentrated effort on your part. Practise this skill until you automatically respond the way you want to. You may find yourself slipping back into your old defensive or retaliatory ways but keep at it. If you do, you'll be able to keep your cool more often when under fire.

How do you deal with Negative Feelings?

Whenever you're having any strong negative feeling, stop to examine whether the feeling is realistic. Every day we're bombarded with negative situations. Examine the list below and determine which of these feelings you have *not* felt in the past month:

Angry; embarrassed; dumb; hurt; intimidated; suspicious; guilty; rejected; troubled; anxious; nervous; uneasy; depressed; distressed; tense; frustrated; concerned; upset; ignored; flustered; emotional; disappointed; humiliated; worried; ashamed; resentful; agitated; jealous; restricted; remorseful; inferior; stupid; offended; insecure; sad; or hindered?

Is there any wonder why many people have become negative-thinking people? So, watch for the physical signs (which you will likely have when faced with people trying to make you feel any of the above), and ask yourself whether you're overreacting. If you've determined that the feeling is not realistic, you've overreacted. This could be ten minutes after the negative situation happened. Turn off your negative reaction - let it go! If you find your mind constantly returning to these negative situations, remind yourself that you're giving someone else control over your life - and don't do it!

The positive approach

I'm sure there have been times when you've had a bad day where everything's gone wrong. You wish you could go back to bed (and it's only 10 a.m.). How you react to this kind of day often determines its outcome. Most people respond by saying *"Oh Boy, it's going to be one of those days!"* They expect the rest of the day to be bad, and, of course it is!

After three or four things have gone wrong in the day, have a talk with yourself. Instead of saying, *"It's going to be one of those days,"* say, *"Thank goodness I got* that *over with."* What you're doing is telling yourself that the rest of the day is going to be better. Try changing to a positive attitude when you're having a bad day and see if it doesn't turn things around.

Positive/Negative Thinking

Positive Thinking: I will succeed because…

Negative Thinking: I will fail because…

Positive Thinking

Attitudes

Understanding
Anticipation
Expectations
Confidence
Patience
Humility
Belief

Behaviour

Enthusiastic
Decisive
Courageous
Optimistic
Cheerful
Considerate
Friendly
Courteous
Warm/Sincere
Relaxed

Results

Success/Security
Recognition

High Energy
Achievement
Happiness/Love
Growth
Adventure
Good Health
Friendship
Inner Peace

Negative thinking

Attitudes

Envy
Greed
Anger
Conceit
Cynicism
Self-Pity
Suspicion
Indecision
Criticism
Inferiority

Behaviour

Lethargic
Indecisive
Timid
Pessimistic
Grumpy
Inconsiderate
Unfriendly
Rude
Weak/Insincere
Irritable
Weak

Results

Worry/Tension
Despondency
Frustration

Job Weariness
Unhappiness
Failure
Poverty/Sickness
Loneliness
Fatigue
Dissatisfaction
Boredom

Now it's time to list all the:

a) Positive-thinking people you associate with on a regular basis.

b) Negative-thinking people you associate with on a regular basis.

c) Percentage of time (in a week) spent with each person.

d) Are you spending more time with positive or negative-thinking people?

e) Are you mainly a positive or negative thinking person?

Are you a Positive or Negative Thinker?

To determine how positive you are, answer these 15 questions as honestly as possible. To score yourself, use the scale listed below:

Always or Almost Always – 4   **Usually – 3**

Sometimes – 2   **Rarely – 1**

Never – 0

_____1. Do you think of yourself as happy?

_____2. Are you surprised when a friend lets you down?

_____3. Do you believe the human race will survive this
century?

_____4. When you think back over the past few months, do you
tend to remember the little successes before your
failures and setbacks?

_____5. If you make a list of your 10 favourite people, would
you be on that list?

_____6. Do you believe that, overall your state of mind has had a positive effect on your physical health?

_____7. Do you feel comfortable making yourself the butt of your own jokes?

_____8. If a policeman stopped you for speeding when you were quite certain you weren't speeding, would you firmly argue your case and take it to court to prove you were right?

_____9. When the unexpected forces you to change your plans, are you quick to spot the hidden advantages in the new situation?

_____10. When you catch a stranger staring at you, do you conclude it's because s/he finds you attractive?

_____11. Do you like most of the people you meet?

_____12. When you think about next year, do you tend to think you'll be better off than you are now?

_____13. Do you often stop to admire things of beauty or interest?

_____14. When someone finds fault with you for something you've done, can you tell the difference between useful (positive) criticism and "griping" (negative) which is better ignored?

_____15. Do you praise your spouse, best friend or lover more often than you criticize him or her?

_____**Total**

Your Score:

49-60 – Excellent – You're a genuine positive-thinker!

44-48 – Good – You're a positive-thinker… usually.

39-43 – Fair – Your positive and negative sides are about evenly matched.

39 and below – Needs Improvement – Netative Pattern. Where do you need to improve?

One woman worked in a very negative workplace. She asked her co-workers to catch her every time she used negative thinking. Soon they were all catching themselves doing so. About a month later their boss called a meeting where he said, *"I don't know what you're doing differently - but keep it up!"*

Unemployed workers should keep in mind that when they are applying for a position - they should be "selling" their skills and abilities - not asking the employer what they can do for them.

Positive thinking requires three pre-requisites:

- Imagination
- The ability to visualize, and
- The belief that you can do it!

Visualization

What does the word visualization mean to you? Many people believe that visualization is the same as having a fantasy. How do the two differ?

Those who fantasize usually aren't in touch with reality. They often try to reach unreachable goals, make a stab at reaching their goal, but stop as soon as they run into resistance. These are often negative thinkers (or become so, because they don't succeed at reaching their fantasy).

The positive thinker who uses visualization, sees themselves reaching their goal, but they also clearly identify obstructions along the way.

Instead of quitting when they hit these barricades, they identify how they can go over, under, around or through the obstacle. Then they identify the next one and so on, until they reach their goal. This is done on paper <u>before</u> their project or goal is underway. If too many obstacles appear, the goal can be dropped without wasting much real effort. (But don't cop out!)

Ways people deal with negative feelings

Many people believe (incorrectly) that bad emotions are always dangerous and powerful. If they express these feelings openly, they tell themselves, they'll lose someone's love or provoke people's anger, boredom or dislike. They can't accept, either, that wanting to be liked by everybody all the time is an unrealistic goal.

On the other side of the scale other people believe (also incorrectly) that it's *"unhealthy"* or *"dishonest"* to try to control how they express their feelings. They believe they have the right to let people know how they feel in any manner they choose; no matter what the circumstances - or the consequences.

To summarise, most people believe there are only two things they can do with their bad emotions: (a) repress them or (b) express them in the form in which they experienced them - that is, negatively. Most of us are also aware that both ways can be destructive.

Avoid Defensiveness in Communicating

Your feelings: Be aware of what you're feeling and how it's affecting the way you're communicating.

Why you feel that way:

If you're becoming uneasy, identify the fact and why you feel that way. Act on this awareness.

Accusing Others:

Avoid accusing others of causing your feelings. No one has control over how you feel or react except you. Use *"I,"* rather than *"You"* statements in conversation when explaining how you feel about something.

Example:

"I feel threatened because it seems that I don't have any control over how I complete my work."

"I feel mistrusted because I don't get a chance to attend the planning session for the work we're expected to do next month."

Confront the issue - not the person:

The issue may however be as a result of the person's behaviour. Focus on the specific incidences rather than make general statements that can't be defended.

Empathy:

Use empathy to understand the other person's needs, values and attitudes.

Timing:

It's imperative to time a confrontation so that the other person is willing to discuss the issue without becoming overly defensive.

Strokes

A stroke is recognition that you get from other people. The fact that you survived, indicates that you have been receiving strokes throughout your life, for you cannot live without them. Strokes can be physical - a hand on the shoulder, an embrace, a handshake, or may be verbal; *"Hello, thank you, well done, or I love you."*

When you were little, someone was there to give you the physical strokes you needed. You were fed, burped and your nose was wiped. all of these were Positive Strokes and with them, came the message *"You're OK."*

Or they could have been negative strokes which say *"You're not OK"* which may have come from sarcastic remarks, destructive discipline, insults or physical punishment.

As you grew up, physical strokes were replaced more and more by verbal ones. Rather than pat you on the head, or hug you, people would say *"Very good"* or *"You did a good job."* Or in the case of negative strokes: *"You're fired."* Or *"You did a lousy job."* Or *"Can't you do anything right?"*

If you're feeling OK, that means that you have probably been getting plenty of good, positive stroking. If you're feeling Not OK, your stroke reserve is low, and you need more positive strokes.

Any time you interact with anyone, strokes are being exchanged. People who give positive strokes are usually fun to be around, and we stay away from people known for giving negative strokes.

Caution #1 - Don't settle for negative strokes

Negative strokes bring feelings of Not OKness, but most people will settle for those, rather than go without strokes. This person says it's better to be kicked , than ignored. The class clown or bully usually falls into this category. Often "good kids" receive little recognition - so revert to negative behaviour. When class clown types get older, they always seem ready for a fight.

Caution #2 - Don't take too many marshmallows

These strokes are often in the form on insincere praise and flattery. These compliments lose value to the receiver because they're not authentic.

The 5 "As"

Acceptance

Attention

Approval

Appreciation

Affection

Expert strokers:

To get to the expert level takes time, planning and practice. You can use these hints to get there:

1. Re-evaluate the social situations you're involved in.

Do they give you OK or Not OK feelings? After you've made this decision, do something about it.

2. Look for new situations where you can get more positive strokes.

Join clubs, church, school, sports, arts, social service groups and volunteer organizations.

3. Don't let positive strokers get away!

Get their names, telephone numbers and some fun information about them. Most importantly, return their positive strokes.

4. Take frequent readings on your own stroke reserve.

If you're running low, go get some positive strokes.

5. Make a "Stroker's" list and keep it current.

This would include people near and far who consistently make you feel OK. Include names, addresses and phone numbers. Keep handy for the times when you're feeling Not OK, or use them to keep you feeling OK about yourself.

6. Get your little OK Kid into action.

This is the laughing, playing part of you. Use it to hook other people's OK Kids and make them feel OK. Make sure your fun is in good taste and appropriate to the situation.

Trading Stamps

Brown stamps:

Brown stamps are collected for bad feelings *"I sure goofed"* and negative strokes from others *"You sure goofed!"* Some, who have collected enough of these, may trade one book of stamps for a free temper tantrum or depression, drug trip, drinking or eating binge. 100 books may be exchanged for a suicide or trip to a mental hospital.

Whenever you feel you've received a negative stroke from someone, try to determine whether they have sent it to you from a parental point of view (parent) where they seemed to look down upon you. Or did they send it from a mature (adult) level where they felt the need to criticize you. Or did they give you the negative stroke from the little kid in them (child) their not OK Kid, because they simply wanted to hurt you.

No one needs to accept brown stamps unless s/he wishes to. To keep from accepting Brown Stamps:

1. State clearly to yourself, *"I hurt."* This is done when you have any Not OK feeling, however slight you may feel. Now describe how you feel, which could be, *"I feel intimidated"* or *"I feel stupid."* Use the phrase which describes your feelings about yourself.

2. Which part of you hurts? It's unlikely that your Adult will hurt, but more likely it will be your Child who has received the hurt. It's possible that some old Parent tape of yours has been trampled on. The part of you that hurts at that particular moment should be recognized.

3. Who did it? Who hurt you? Was it YOU that hurt YOU? *"I should have known better than that!"* or was it someone else?

4. Which part of the other person did it? Was it their Parent, Adult or Child?

5. Why did the other person give you this hurt? Was it accidental? Was it on purpose? What was the reason that the particular statement was made, and what made it hurt?

6. What can you do now, instead of collecting a Brown Stamp? What can you do differently the next time you meet another person who says or does the same thing?

Gold stamps:

Gold Stamps are good feelings, *"I sure did a good job that time!"* collected from experiences such as winning, achieving or anything that brings au-thentic Positive Strokes.

When Gold Stamps are cashed in, the prize may be a relaxing vacation, an enjoyable celebration or new clothes. These are the stamps that you should strive to pass on to others. Hook the other person's OK Kid, and make them laugh!

CHAPTER TWO

WHY COMMUNICATION BREAKS DOWN

Logic versus emotion: the analytical approach

If negative emotions go in, they must get out somehow. We have seen some of the instinctive ways people deal with them. Most of these instinctive and/or impulsive reactions have negative consequences. The challenge is to find ways to deal with negative emotions constructively.

Two forces - logic and emotion - are at work throughout our lives. Often, they push and pull in opposite directions. The one that prevails at any time, will determine how we get along with others and may affect our level of achievement. We all know it's easy to respond to situations with emotions rather than logic but responding logically helps us deal constructively with difficult circumstances.

If it does not come naturally to you to behave logically under stress, don't be discouraged. The ability to use logic to resolve conflicts and problems can be developed. The first step is to gain some insight into the nature of the difficulty. You can do this by analysing the situation, your feelings and your behaviour. Armed with information from this analysis, you can then learn to take charge of your reactions instead of letting your instincts control you.

Here are two examples that show how the analytical approach could be useful.

1. Suppose you feel depressed for no other reason than because it's a Monday morning. Do you phone in sick, or do you try to figure out what's wrong? When you analyse your reactions, you realise that you regularly have an upper on Friday afternoon and a downer on Monday morning. You may be one of the 80 per cent of employed people who are in the wrong job. Do you let that depress you further, or do you do the logical thing and seriously consider looking for suitable employment?

When you consider that most of us spend ten hours a day, five days a week either getting ready for, travelling to, or in the workplace, it's a shame that people don't spend more energy deciding what they would like to do with their lives. If you find yourself in the wrong job or occupation and decide to look for something you enjoy more, you could start by contacting a vocational guidance centre (they are listed in the telephone book).

2. Suppose you are under pressure to finish a job by 2:00 p.m., when your supervisor suddenly gives you an extra batch of work. Because your supervisor often does this, you find you regularly have difficulty completing your allocated work on time. This makes you feel inadequate. On the other hand, you don't want to annoy your supervisor and end up at 2:00 p.m. having to say, *"I'm sorry, I haven't finished it yet?"* Or do you say, *"I won't have time to complete this and the Jones report by 2:00 p.m. Which would you rather I do?"*

    In the first case, your supervisor is angry with you anyway, because, by not speaking up, you prevented her from making other arrangements for completing the report. You then complain saying, *"My job makes me feel that I'm under a lot of pressure."*

    In the second case, your analysis of such situations has made you realise that it is your supervisor's responsibility to help you make priorities. To ensure she can do this effectively, you make sure you have a good idea of your present workload. Perhaps you have taken a time-management course to help you choose your priorities. You keep *"to do"* lists, so you know exactly how much you can handle in a day, and you are careful to keep your supervisor informed of your workload.

Analysing stress

Certain physical and behavioural symptoms are associated with stress. Besides the flight-or-fight symptoms mentioned earlier, stress shows its pressure through:

- Heightened sensitivity to noise
- Racing thoughts
- Impatience
- Restlessness
- Sudden rages
- Bouts of laughing or weeping.

In some cases, depression and apathy may also be reactions to stress. Not all stress is bad. The heightened emotions and physical symptoms associated with stress can occur in response to pleasurable or exciting events - such as being promoted or being in love. It's not stress that's the problem, then but negative stress - the kind that produces *dis*tress.

For example, most people assume that workaholics are unhappy, but that's not always true. There are two basic kinds of workaholic. There are those who love their jobs and work hard and long because they receive pleasure from doing so. They're under stress but seldom suffer from *dis*tress. Other workaholics are motivated not by enthusiasm but by such things as:

- Competitive feelings;
- Job pressures;
- Budget cuts;
- Family or relationship problems;
- Financial problems.

Their stress becomes *dis*tress and they suffer because of it. We all know these people. They:

- Work all the time, often bringing work home in the evenings and on weekends - but are resentful about it;
- Suffer from nervous disorders;
- Don't eat or exercise properly;

- Never take time off from work when they're ill (they're the ones who pass on the flu bug to the rest of the staff because they come in when they shouldn't);

- Seldom spend time with the family;

- Don't know how to relax or play or simply do nothing. (They often use competitive sports to relax.)

Stress becomes *dis*tress when we've been under pressure too long or the pressures in life become overwhelming. The first step in dealing with *dis*tress is to analyse all the sources of stress in your life to determine first, which sources are positive, and which are negative, and second, which sources you can do something about, and which you can't change. To do this, go through the following exercise as accurately as you can. Write down your answers; don't just go through the exercise mentally.

1) On a sheet of paper, list everything that's causing you stress. (Leave space between each stressor.) Try to give at least five stressors.

2) On a scale of 1 to 10 (10 being the highest) determine the stress level of each stressor.

3) Determine if the stressor is positive (a wedding, a promotion, a new baby, a new job) or negative (rudeness, driving in rush-hour traffic).

4) Put down the feelings you have in the stressful situation (anger, frustration, happiness, fear) next to each stressor.

5) Identify which part of your life is most affected by each negative stressor (family, social, business/work).

6) Then for each stressor determine whether:

   a) You *DO* have the power to alleviate the problem. Put the word *DO* next to the item; or:

   b) You *DON'T* have the power to change the situation. It's beyond your control - there's nothing you can do about it. Put the word *DON'T* next to the item.

Techniques for Reducing Negative Stress (distress)

Once you have identified the negative sources of stress in your life and have determined which of them you could do something about, you're well on the way to obtaining relief from the worst pressures.

Two more steps should then follow your analysis:

1. If you *DON'T* have the power to do something about a negative source of stress, forget about it. Mentally throw the problem away and don't waste any more precious energy thinking about it.

2. If you *DO* have the power to change the situation, think about what you are going to do about it. Draw up a plan of action.

These steps put the **Serenity Prayer** (written by Reinhold Niebuhr) into practice:

> *"God grant me the serenity to accept the things I cannot change, the courage to change the things I can, and the wisdom to know the difference."*

One of my seminar participants identified the following problem that involved road rage: *"My personal annoyance is rush-hour traffic. Almost every day, I get into a bad mood watching the stupid things other drivers do."*

This is probably one of the things in your life that you have no control over. What you do have control over is your reaction to it. Drive defensively. Remind yourself not to get upset. Use your favourite radio station or play a tape you enjoy. You might consider travelling earlier or later to miss traffic jams.

The Way to Win Arguments

Nobody likes to lose an argument. Here are clues to how you might win your next one:

1. Ask for time to think things over. Then both of you can take this opportunity to calm down.

2. Pay attention to your body's reaction. Has the fight-or-flight reaction been triggered? Take a deep breath to increase your oxygen intake to your brain so it can analyse your situation more clearly.

3. Don't snap back at the person. You may regret a fast retort, which may have lasting repercussions.

4. Determine what it is you want that you're not getting? Should you be willing to negotiate more - to give in a little so you can both win?

5. If the other person has *"lost it"*, don't negotiate until s/he's calmed down. A quiet manner is always your best approach.

6. Wait until s/he's willing to listen to your side of the story. Make sure you're listening carefully to his/her side of the story.

7. Make sure s/he knows you're listening. Use paraphrasing on a regular basis to confirm that what s/he's said is what you heard.

8. S/he doesn't seem to be listening to what you have to say. Insist that s/he does. Say, *"I've made a point of listening carefully to what you have to say. Can I count on you to do the same for me?"*

9. Ask, *"What do you want me to do?"* Clarify that you know what s/he wants. Listen to his/her answer and confirm or correct.

10. State what you want, clearly and sequentially. Again, be willing to negotiate.

11. When an agreement is reached, summarise the agreement and go over pertinent areas again to re-confirm your understanding.

Games People Play

Manipulative behaviour is displayed in many ways. I'll briefly discuss nineteen kinds of behaviour. Please try to think of examples of them as I go along.

These *"games"* as we define them, are manipulative and dishonest. They use indirect and unclear communication. Often the person *"playing the game"* is not even aware that they're doing so.

(Note: I'll be using *"she"* in my examples)

You may receive more detailed explanations of these games by reading my book **Dealing with Difficult People.** Chapter 2 of my book discusses the 115 ways people try to manipulate others and how to deal with them.

Here are some of the "Games people play" to make you do what they want you to do:

Game #1 - The Sufferer: (Or, *"After all I've done for you!"*) (Passive resistance).

The sufferer gets what she wants by sending indirect messages. She may play the part of the martyr, act overworked, persecuted or totally dependent. She sighs a lot and utters indirect complaints. She's trying to say, *"If you appreciated me, or even noticed all the things I do for you - you'd want to do more for me!"*

Game #2 - Uninvolved: (Or, *"It doesn't matter to me - whatever you want."*) (Passive resistance).

Here's an example of a telephone conversation:

John: *"Are you busy tonight? How about a movie?"*

Alice: (hesitating) *"Well, I guess that's okay."* (She'd been planning on doing some shopping after work, then coming home and washing her hair). *"Yes, that would be fun I suppose."* (weakly).

John: *"What would you like to see?"*

Alice: *"Oh, it doesn't make any difference to me."*

John: *"We could see the new science fiction downtown, or that new western at the varsity..."*

Alice: *"Whichever you prefer."* (She hates westerns).

John: *I don't feel like driving all the way downtown – so let's go to the western.*

Alice: (after a long pause followed by a sigh) *"Well... okay."*

John: *"Are you sure that's what you want?"*

Alice: *"It really doesn't matter much... Whichever you like..."* Etc.

The deliberately uninvolved person is never wrong - but is never right either. However, it's okay to say *"It doesn't matter to me"* if that's the truth.

Game #3 - *"I won't fight:"*   (But I won't give in either!) (Passive resistance)

Helen lives in the household of her son Bob and daughter-in-law Emily. Emily wants to re-decorate their family room by purchasing woven basket chairs with big pillows that could be used as well for sitting on the floor in front of the fireplace. Helen (the mother-in-law) prefers a comfortable couch.

Emily: *"Some of those fabrics on the pillows I saw yesterday are beautiful."*

Helen: *"Are they cotton?"*

Emily: *"Yes, they are."*

Helen: *"They'll probably shrink when you wash them... and they'll show the dirt."*

Emily: *"Well maybe we could look for other kinds of fabric and cover them ourselves."*

Helen: *"That should be done professionally. Besides, anything that sits around on the floor will start looking terrible soon."* (wearily). *"But if that's what you want - get them."*

Emily: *"Well, I like big pillows. Is there anything you particularly want?"*

Helen: *"Not exactly. Furniture should be sensible and made to last. But it's your home. Do what you like. I can always sit in the living room."*

Later, Helen reported to a friend that she wasn't the kind of mother who bothered her children with her opinions. Yet Helen didn't support anyone else's ideas unless they happened to be the same as hers.

Game #4 - Saboteur: *("I'll go through the motions, but I"ll fight you every step of the way")*. (also Passive resistant).

For example: Don says: *"My wife wants me to clean the basement this weekend. I'm going to give it a stab but won't clean it to her standards. Then maybe she won't expect me to do that job again."*

The office secretary makes horrible coffee because she doesn't drink coffee and objects to making it for others.

A husband comes home late too often for dinner – so wife leaves his dinner to dry out in the oven.

Game #5 – Fear Victim: (Allow fear to control their lives).

The fear victim is so ruled by anxiety and fear that it arouses, that s/he avoids the situation and thus avoids assertiveness. A university study showed that, of the things people fear:

- 40% never happen
- 30% are things that happened in the past
- 22% are needless, petty, small
- 8% are real, but divided into:
  - o Those they can solve
  - o Those they can't solve

Examples:
  - o Agoraphobics. These people have panic attacks when they even attempt to leave their homes.
  - o Fear of fire, heights, spiders etc.

Game #6 – Sham Assertive: (Pretend to be assertive).

This person pretends to be assertive. They may seem open, warm and even extroverted, but this covers for a lack of honesty. This person would state *"How wonderful to hear from you - I was just thinking about you."* (Completely untrue - you know she detests you). People in this category have problems in any but the most superficial relationships.

Game #7 – Everyone must love me! (Or they feel they're a failure.)

Their goal is to have everyone, spouse lover, children, boss, friends, shopkeepers and even the man who comes to the door selling magazines to think they're the greatest.

Game #8 – Split Assertive: (Different behaviour styles determined by the situation.

They use different behaviour styles that are determined by the situation. This person may be a tiger on the job and a mouse in an intimate relationship or vice versa.

Game #9 – Procrastinator: (Puts things off).

These people always have excuses as to why a job isn't done. They say, *"I'll do it tomorrow"* which may or may not come to pass.

Game 10 - Always Late: (Disrupts others.)

This person is late for events s/he doesn't want to attend or isn't ready when others are. They often disrupt meetings, social events, concerts and generally is lacking in consideration for other's valuable time.

See which type of person you are. There is a 10:00 a.m. meeting. You arrive at:

a) 10:00 a.m.

b) You must be early for everything, so you arrive at 9:45 a.m.

c) You arrive at 10:10 a.m.

The a) people are cutting it a little fine. People should be five or ten minutes early for appointments so they can prepare for it.

The b) s might waste a lot of their time unless they bring something to do during the extra time.

c)s make others angry because by their lateness, they are telling those that are already there that *their* time isn't important.

Game #11 - Always Slow: (Need others to motivate them.)

Sure, their report is ready - but it took them so long to prepare it, the boss felt like taking the job on him/herself. These people are usually low energy people who appear to be *putting in time* - are existing rather than living - usually in positions they don't like. They can drive other, more organized people to distraction.

Game #12 - Sloppy or Careless: (Habit)

The work is done so poorly, that someone else must re-do the effort which often takes more time than the original task.

Game #13 - Forgetfulness or Neglect: (Expect others to remind them.)

Their usual comment is *"I forgot"* or *"Why didn't you remind me to do that?"* They don't meet deadlines or know who is responsible for what project *"Oh, I thought you were looking after that!"*

Game #14 – Sarcasm (Indirect aggression)

Some sarcasm is nothing more than harmless kidding. It is non-threatening and can be fun. However, sarcasm can also be hurtful, designed to make others feel small. People using it feel a sense of power at seeing other people squirm. Hurtful sarcasm is a form of indirect aggression – one of the sneakiest, most manipulative and underhanded methods of getting your way.

People who use hurtful sarcasm often don't feel very good about themselves, so they attempt to put others down to make themselves feel more important. The game continues when others respond defensively, or act hurt. Sarcastic people want others to get angry and defend themselves. Remind yourself not to respond negatively to their remarks. Try to stick to the facts.

Think for a minute; who's in control in the situation when sarcasm is used? You are (the recipient of the sarcasm) until you reply. Should you respond to sarcasm with more sarcasm? No. If you do, you often just encourage more of the same. Instead, try to analyse why the person might feel the need to put you down. Once you have an idea of what really prompts the sarcasm, you'll be able to deal with the actual issue.

Don't react to sarcasm - turn it off. The sarcastic person won't know what to do, because you're not playing by "the rules."

When it's no longer fun to throw things at you, the culprit will take his or her sarcastic remarks elsewhere.

If you can't stay quiet, and feel that the sarcasm warrants a response, you might say,

"Your last comment was very sarcastic, and a put-down. Put-downs hurt. Can you explain why you said what you did?" Or,

"Why do you feel you have to give me a put-down like that?" Or,

"That was pretty sarcastic. What is it that you really want to say to me that you're covering up with sarcasm?"

Make aggressive people account for their actions. Often, they aren't aware of how destructive their behaviour is to others.

For example: Jane says: *"I see you finally made the decision to get your hair cut in a style that suits you."*

Make aggressive people account for their actions. Often, they aren't aware of how destructive their behaviour is to others.

When I was doing the research for my book, *Escaping the Pink-Collar Ghetto* (now entitled *The Business Women's Bible*) I interviewed more than 700 managers (695 of them men) to see why they weren't promoting more women. Initially, I was met with a crossed-arms defensive stance from most of the managers. I knew they were on the defensive when the sarcasm started to flow. My instinctive reaction was to fight sarcasm with sarcasm, but instead, I stood back from the situation and tried to analyse it. I concluded that these managers felt that when I asked, *"Why aren't you promoting more women?"* that I was accusing them of discriminatory behaviour.

I reassured them by explaining fully what I was there to accomplish; that I really needed their input to find out what "mistakes" women were making that kept them from being promoted. I gave several examples other companies had given me and asked them if the same was true in their company as well. Soon they realised that I was there only to obtain information and their help, not to push them into defending the scarcity of women in senior positions in their company. Most were then very cooperative. They would not have been, however, if I had responded defensively to their sarcasm.

Game # 15 – Ignoring, the silent treatment or sulking (indirect aggression).

Another form of indirect aggression is ignoring others, sulking or giving them the silent treatment by refusing to discuss important issues with them. Some supervisors even refuse to speak to a staff member about anything for days even though they're members of the same department! This is dirty pool and almost as destructive as vindictive sarcasm.

This negative action is a no-win situation for both parties involved. Often the person giving the silent treatment wins the battle but prolongs the war. If issues are not settled through discussion, they will inevitably resurface later.

For example: Linda hadn't spoken to her husband Bill for four days following an argument. They hadn't resolved the issue, and Bill had tried several times to get her to talk about the problem. She refused.

Brian felt proud when his department head commended him in front of his co-workers and supervisor for the excellent job he had done on a project. Brian had worked hard to complete the project and felt he deserved the praise. Later that day, he asked his supervisor, Harry, for technical advice relating to his newest project. Harry was very abrupt and told him to figure it out himself. During the next week, Brian received the cold shoulder from Harry, who wasn't as available or supportive as usual. Brian decided to speak to Harry. He said, *"I have a problem and I need your help in solving it."* He used feedback to explain how he felt when Harry withdrew his help and asked him to explain why this was happening.

Harry admitted that he was upset when Brian received praise from the department head, and that he felt jealous because this had never happened to him in the past. He promised to be more available in the future.

Game #16 - Sticky Iffies (Backhanded compliments)

These are backhanded compliments. They start by praising you and end up with a qualifying put-down. These left-handed compliments catch you off guard the first time. You feel so good about the praise that you didn't realise until later that there was a hidden negative implication tied to it. A little later, you wonder if you just imagined the slap - or if it was really intended. The two-sided remark was meant as a barb. Trying not to show signs of being stung, you feel yourself smile and hear yourself sputter thanks, while knowing that's not the way you should respond. Then you kick yourself for having thanked somebody who just got away with putting you down. Examples of this are:

"You can lift a lot of weight for someone so small."

"You're in great shape for a person your age."

"You're almost as smart as your sister."

"You make a lot of money for a woman."

"You're really agile for a person your size."

To overcome:

1. *Divide the remark into two parts - praise and put-down.*

2. *Reply to the person, "I don't know how you expect me to react to your last comment. On one hand you've given me a compliment, then you've pulled the rug out from under me by giving me a put-down. Which way did you intend me to receive it?"* (This makes the person know that you're onto their game playing.)

Game #17 – Gossip

They're rumourmongers who spread unverified or expanded stories. Their intent is to gain attention for themselves by spreading untrue or partly true messages. They often embroider the story, filling in the blanks to make it appear more important or believable or how they think it *"should be"*. They forget details, remembering only vivid parts and distorting the facts by omitting vital information.

Jill: *"Did you hear about Carmen's husband? He was picked up for drunk-driving last night."*

Game #18 - Temper tantrums.

These are childish, inappropriate, and uncontrolled expressions of anger that can be triggered by anything - some trivial current event or something that took place long ago that the person has stewed about for years. People who are prone to temper tantrums may deal with minor irritations of day-to-day life by saying nothing at the time, then, when a chance remark acts as a trigger, they can erupt in a red flash of rage and lash out at the nearest person. This fury has unfortunate consequences; the person feels terrible and others are alienated. This person needs professional anger management.

Adult tantrums are designed to cope with feelings of fear, helplessness and frustration. To a child, tantrums are a great equalizing mechanism. Such disruptive behaviour continues into adulthood, if the outbursts still work. However, tantrums produce a greater backwash of anger and resistance than any of the other difficult behaviours. Coping with a person having a tantrum is chiefly a matter of helping them regain self-control.

Agree to Disagree

There are times when you'll find yourself in a conversation with others and recognise that you're on opposite sides of the issue. For instance: abortion, gun control, politics, religion and euthanasia. Neither of you will budge an inch and both parties become more and more upset because the other can't see things from their perspective.

This is especially trying for people who have great respect and admiration for each other. It's important to recognise that no two people (no matter how close they are) can think the same way about every issue in life. They are not traitors (as each might feel the other is) should they have differing views.

Whenever you find yourself in this kind of situation say, *"You're entitled to your opinion and so am I. It's obvious that we're never going to agree on this issue, so let's agree to disagree, and not talk about this in the future."* If the person insists on continuing with the argument, refuse to participate in the discussion. If s/he brings the issue up later, remind him/her that you will not budge in your opinion, so it's unwise to get heated up about the issue again.

Being Constructive

Of course, it is sometimes necessary to discuss people's mistakes - in other words, to criticise them. Criticism can be either *destructive* - making the person feel worthless - or *constructive* - offering specific suggestions for improvement. When criticising others, always correct the person's behaviour. Don't give them labels such as dumb, stupid, lazy, sloppy, ignorant, or uncaring. People don't know how to improve these things, and using such terms just brings out retaliation in the person receiving the comment.

Think about the last rip-snorting argument you had with someone. Did you label the *person,* or did you play fair and discuss the person's *behaviour?*

For example, you could say: *"John, you didn't spend much time preparing your report, did you? It turned out to be useless, and I had to do it over again."* That's discussing his behaviour and giving him specific information about how he can change it.

In an argument, if you found yourself labelling someone, please apologise to him or her. Say, *"I'm sorry. You didn't deserve that. What I meant to say was..."* You then discuss the behaviour that offended you.

If people label you, ask for specific reasons why they have given you the label. Remember, you have the choice of accepting or not accepting the criticism.

We can decide not to allow people to hurt us. A co-worker may betray us, gossip about us, or try to make us feel guilty. It's not easy to forgive this behaviour. We may feel that we're letting ourselves down if we forgive others too easily. We may feel we should wait for them to do something to mend the rift. We may be tempted to dwell to an unhealthy extent on the injury we feel they have done us.

In many cases, however, forgiving is the only thing that will mend and heal. Forgiving can lead to a renewed relationship. You may say, *"That's easy for you to say! Your co-worker didn't gossip behind your back and pass on untrue information about you."*

Here's what you can do to mend the rift. Stop pretending that you like the person. Acknowledge to yourself that you are angry and examine why. Then be direct with the other person, telling him or her frankly what has offended you. Keep in mind, however, that the person is only human, and that we all make mistakes. Then make a conscious decision to forgive and forget. (You need to mean it.) Once you have forgiven the person, you can get on with your life.

Many people don't agree with this approach. They believe that forgiving wrongdoers just lets them off the hook - it's too easy on the wrongdoer. Anger and hate use up energy that should be spent positively on picking up the pieces.

I found that I could get on with my life when I forgave others for injuries done to me. Ironically, in my case, all these people have subsequently had problems resulting directly from their own hurtful behaviour. For instance, one boss I had was afraid that I might be after his job. He made my life a living hell for months, which caused terrible stress and health problems for me. I finally had to admit defeat and look for work elsewhere. That man is now bouncing from one job to another, each at a lower level than the one before. He leaves behind a string of former co-workers who despise him.

Giving Criticism

We come from a critical society and appear far more able to accept criticism than praise. Our own worst critic appears to be ourselves.

If you have to criticize another person, give constructive, rather than destructive criticism. You don't want to make them feel as if they must defend themselves. Instead of saying, *"You made a mistake."* say, *"The next time you do this, I'd like you to do it this way."*

Constructive Criticism:

You attempt to correct the behaviour of the person:

"Jack, I can't use the figures you gave me for the Miller report, because they were last year's figures."

Destructive Criticism:

You criticize the person - not their behaviour by using labels such as: *Dumb, Stupid, Sloppy, Careless, Uncaring, Destructive* or the worst one for children, *"Bad."* For example:

"Jack, you ruined the Miller report. I can't believe you could be so dumb!"

If destructive criticism is given, the person feels the need to defend themselves (because you HAVE attacked them), and their behaviour will most likely continue. Constructive criticism identifies the behaviour that's offending you, and gives the person a chance to correct his/her behaviour.

Receiving Criticism

When others criticize you:

1. Control your thoughts and behaviour.

2. Don't retaliate - listen carefully to their comments.

3. Ask for specifics if criticism is vague.

4. Confirm your understanding of the problem (using paraphrasing).

5. If criticism is valid - apologize. Let them know what steps you will take to correct the behaviour or problem. Realize mentally that this failure or problem is part of life and that you should not expect perfection from yourself. You should strive not to repeat this failure or cause the problem again.

6. When dealing with a client, and the problem or behaviour being criticized is NOT your fault - mentally confirm this with yourself. Think, *"I'm not responsible for that problem, but I'll help them solve it."* and don't accept the criticism as being valid.

For Example:

A client calls to blame you for poor delivery of your company's products. As you are the accountant, you have no responsibility for delivery, therefore, if you mentally refuse to accept the negative, you can keep your cool and gear your energies towards solving their problem. Say, *"Let's see what I can do to help solve this problem."*

You keep your cool, and so does the client. Both win - nobody loses.

Who's perfect?

Improper Criticism of others:

Threats: This also provokes retaliation.

Shame or Blame: Most people shame or blame others and generalize. When statements begin with *"never"* or *"always,"* it invites retaliation.

Faulty feedback: The criticizer's feedback is vague, which is worse than no feedback at all. The person doesn't know what's the problem which provokes the *"Yes but ... "* response.

Productive critical feedback:

a. Gives us the opportunity of hearing what others think about us.

b. Helps us see our own mistakes.

c. Makes us think about alternatives.

d. Stops repeat mistakes.

Before you criticize - determine:

1. Which behaviour do you want to change?

2. Can it be changed?

3. Is this the time and the place to discuss it (privacy)?

When giving Criticism:

1. Use "I" statements.

2. Ask for feedback (ask questions).

3. Commit yourself (be supportive).

After giving criticism:

1. Follow through.

2. Reward any favourable behaviour change.

When receiving criticism:

1. Hear it.

2. Understand it.

3. Summarize it.

4. Evaluate it.

Stop yourself if you find yourself automatically finding ways to defend yourself. There might be some truth in what the person is saying.

Accepting compliments

Many of us have difficulty receiving compliments graciously. We discount or refuse to accept them with such comments as, *"Oh, I could have done better,"* or *"This old rag?"*

If you don't accept compliments graciously, what are you telling the person giving you the compliment? You are implying that s/he is insincere, has poor judgement or even worse - is lying. You repaid a warm-fuzzy (a good feeling) with a cold-prickly (a bad feeling). Remember this the next time you discount a compliment.

CHAPTER THREE

COMMUNICATING WITH OTHERS

What Kind of Person are You?

Before we learn how to manage others, important for you to identify not only your personality style, but also that of other people, especially if you're having problems dealing with them. We can change how we deal with others, so we'll be more on their "wave length" and can match their communication needs. We're all a mixture of these four personality types, but one should match more clearly than the others. To do this:

Personality types

From the information given below, (reading only the strengths and descriptions below each type) choose the personality type closest to your behaviour pattern. This will require you to look inside yourself to determine what you feel and do in *"real life."*

Strengths

Type A: Strengths:

Direct; outgoing; up-front; stimulating; people skilled; persuasive; risk-taker; persuasive; competitive and self-assured.

These people are spontaneous, often employed in sales, are people-people - they want respect from others. Others may feel they're aggressively competitive in their pursuit of what they want. They dislike people who lack enthusiasm, keep them waiting, are indecisive or rigid, or those who go by the book. They love attention, a sense of achievement, and crave recognition, adventure and excitement.

Type B: Strengths:

Practical; ambitious; efficient; methodical; direct; results-oriented; conventional; resolute; determined; organised and dependable.

These people make good entrepreneurs and directors. They like to direct and take charge of things. They're task-oriented and must always win. They hate emotional people, ambiguity, disrespect and laziness in others. They like others to be controlled, loyal, to keep a fast pace, and like responsibility.

Type C: Strengths:

Team-oriented; warm; faithful; enthusiastic; cooperative; approachable; trusting; sensitive; good listener; good friend; likes change; is outgoing and ambassador.

These people are often in the service industry (hospitality, health care, transportation, social services) because they have a strong desire to help others. They hold in stress and store it away - seldom putting themselves first. They're protective of the underdog, want everyone to love them, and are often passive in their behaviour. They dislike insensitive, argumentative, insincere or egotistical people. They like others who are warm, kind and caring.

Type D: Strengths:

Rigid; meticulous; accurate; inhibited; painstaking; sensible; serene; high standards; avoids risks.

These are more detail-oriented than people-people. They enjoy working alone, often in accounting, technical, or engineering fields. They dislike people who are fakes, overly assertive, careless or arrogant. They like those who are perfectionists, consistent, informed, practical, good workers, are easy to get along with.

Weaknesses

Now look at the weaknesses of your chosen personality type. These are typical weaknesses for the types of personalities and can make YOU a difficult person to others. You may have eliminated many of these negative traits, but you'll likely recognise many that you'll need to work on.

Type A: Weaknesses:

Browbeater; domineering; restless; impatient; pushy; manipulative; grating; reactive and controlling.

Type B: Weaknesses:

Uncaring; critical; frugal; unyielding; aloof; uncompromising; distant; insistent; stubborn; inflexible and inaccessible.

Type C: Weaknesses:

Too empathetic; indecisive; unreasonable; defenceless; wishy-washy; subjective; hesitant; irrational; vulnerable; pushover; passive; pleases others and get walked-on.

Type D: Weaknesses:

Procrastinates; perfectionist; unsociable; uninteresting; brooding; bashful; passive; hates change and monotonous.

Do everything you can to try to correct the weaknesses you have that make you a difficult person to others.

Then analyse the information to determine the personality of the difficult people you must deal with. This requires a high degree of empathy - you'll have to place yourself in their shoes to come up with an accurate analysis of your difficult people.

List your difficult people giving their name. Then determine their personality type from the earlier information.

Next determine what adjustments you should take to adapt your communication style to make it more in tune with that of your difficult people. (To do this, you need to be willing to adapt your personality style to come closer to theirs. Remember you likely *can't* change their behaviour, but you *can* change your reaction to their behaviour.)

How to work with other personality types

If you're in a working or personal relationship with someone of these types, here are a few things that may be helpful to remember:

A Type

- Give praise, credit and recognition regularly.
- Be sociable with them.
- Treat them as if what they're doing is important.
- Encourage them to use their creative abilities.
- If they're hyperactive, re-channel their energies - help them choose priorities.

B Type

- Give them as much control as possible.
- Give loose supervision - lots of rope.
- Make them feel important.
- Utilize their efficient, practical and ambitious nature.
- Use their organisational abilities.
- Respect their conventional values and methods.
- Be flexible in accepting their way of doing things.

C Type

- Don't get upset with their need to have everyone like them.
- Treat others even more fairly when in their presence.
- Be up-front in your dealings with them.
- Give them opportunities to mingle with others.
- Have patience with their indecisive behaviour.

D Type

- Listen to their ideas.
- Help them set deadlines.
- Give them room to do the job their way.
- Use logic and facts in discussions.
- Show respect.

If your **supervisor or manager** is from one of these types, consider these guidelines:

A Type

- Be sociable with them.
- Give them lots of credit.
- Help them interact with others.
- Help them see things in a realistic light.
- Show enthusiasm and excitement.
- Be up-front in communication.
- Feed their ego.
- Be open and friendly.
- Be outgoing, not shy with them.

B Type

- Document everything.
- Be results-oriented.
- Respect their authority.
- Give them challenges.
- Follow rules and regulations.
- Be punctual. Keep to the point.
- Be a buffer between them and other employees.
- Help them see alternative ways of doing things.

C Type

- Show you're interested in them and what they do.
- Offer support.
- Express thoughts and ideas freely.
- Be a team player, willing to compromise.
- Help them communicate with others.
- Set your own objectives and complete them.

D Type

- Give detailed hard facts and data.
- Acknowledge their proficiency.
- Be consistent.
- Document ideas, giving facts to back them up.
- Offer new ideas and approaches.

Look at the *"Working with Type As, Bs, Cs and Ds"* and see how you could get along better with others. It's often impossible to get others to adapt their personality to match ours, so it's up to us to try to adapt to theirs.

How could you improve your communication with them?

Introvert and Extrovert Personality Types

It's important to analyse where your difficult people fit in relation to their wants, needs and desires. Analyse your difficult person - see how you can more effectively deal with their difficult behaviour by evaluating where they fit in the following three categories:

Extreme introvert:

This is an extremely careful person, is contemplative and analytical, leans toward perfectionism, and can work doggedly at detailed work. Introverts tend to be a "cerebral" type of person concerned with affairs of the mind rather than a lot of physical activity.

Extreme extrovert:

This person is more action-oriented, prefers to get started quickly, deciding on details along the way (or ignoring them altogether, thinking someone else will take care of them). Extroverts may get many things started but leave some details unfinished.

Combination introvert/extrovert: This person combines some attributes of both the introvert and the extrovert and is a balance of the two extremes. Their individual actions would tell you which phase they are in at that time.

Common ways extreme Introverts feel and behave:

- Don't like to lend things to others. They'll do it, but with much hesitancy and caution.
- Would rather make a report in writing than give it verbally.
- Can be very blunt and straightforward.
- Are more reserved in their laughter or other displays of feelings and emotion.
- Are very careful with their personal possessions. Keep things looking nice and in good order.
- Are slow in action and decision-making.
- Are very sensitive about comments made about them.
- Become embarrassed quite easily.
- Considered perfectionists by many. Write and rewrite until everything's perfect.
- Are chronic worriers.
- Are quite concerned and deliberate about most routine decisions.
- Resent autocratic commands from others.
- Can be extreme in religion, politics and other social issues.
- Tend to struggle alone with problems.
- Quite comfortable working alone, rather than as a member of a team.
- Enjoy and need praise and recognition but won't ask for it.
- Tend to be suspicions.
- Are moodier than a strong extrovert.
- Enjoy work requiring precision and attention to detail.
- Prefer intellectual pursuits.
- Daydream a lot and think about what might have been or what is yet to come.

- Are extremely conscientious and berate themselves for less than perfect performances.

Common ways extreme Extroverts feel and behave:

- Lend money and possessions readily.
- Fluent talkers; can give reports better orally than in writing.
- Usually careful not to hurt others' feelings and want to be liked by others.
- Laugh readily.
- Don't take care of personal possessions.
- Make decisions quickly.
- Are quick in their actions. Seldom rewrite letters or give attention to detail.
- Hard to embarrass.
- Are quick in their actions. Seldom rewrite letters or give attention to detail.
- Aren't worriers.
- Aren't bothered by details of what to wear, what to eat, where to go, etc.
- Aren't very concerned by what's said about them.
- Accept orders as a matter of course.
- Are usually moderate in their religion, politics and other social issues.
- Don't hesitate to ask for help in solving problems.
- Would rather work with others than alone.
- Make their own opportunities for praise.
- Aren't suspicious of others' motives.
- Are in about the same mood always.
- Prefer work where details are not important.
- Prefer athletics to books and *"high-brow"* activities.
- Are not great planners - take things as they come.

- Are risk-takers and gamblers - seldom worry about the consequences.

Approaches to Conflict Resolution

We have seen that many conflicts and resentments arise because people feel either that they need to defend themselves against an aggressor or that they have inadvertently taken advantage of a too-passive person. The ability to behave assertively rather than aggressively or passively can significantly reduce the level of conflict and stress in your life. However, conflicts cannot be avoided entirely. When they do arise, the principles of assertive behaviour that are so effective for preventing conflicts are also helpful for resolving them.

Following are basic approaches to solving conflicts:

1. *Competition.* One person or group wins, while the other group loses.

2. *Accommodation.* One person refuses even to state his or her wishes, but simply goes along with the other's statements or demands.

3. *Compromise/collaboration.* Each person recognizes the other's rights. Each may need to yield on some points, but it is understood that the solution must consider the needs and wishes of both.

There are no competitive feelings in the last approach. Instead, there is a feeling of cooperation or camaraderie among the participants. This attitude uses each person's talents and recognises each person's rights.

Styles of Behaviour and Their Effects

To a large extent, your ability to deal *constructively* with stress, anger and difficult situations depends on the *style of behaviour* you most readily adopt. Here are six basic behavioural styles and the behaviours that go along with them:

Assertive Behaviour

- Respect for one's self - expressing one's needs and defending one's rights.

- Respect for the other person's needs and rights.

Passive Behaviour

- No respect for oneself.
- Does not express one's needs.
- Does not defend one's rights.

Aggressive Behaviour

- Respect for one's self - expressing one's needs and defending one's rights.
- No respect for the other person's needs and rights.

Passive Resistance

These are passive people who are trying to become more assertive in their behaviour. They mutter and sigh a lot and play manipulative games to get their way. They have not learned to ask up-front for what they want. The following scenario is an example:

Joey: *"Mom, can you drive me to school today?"*

His mother had her morning planned. It was a beautiful day, and Joey as usual had been fooling around until he was late for school.

Mom: *"Joey, I've driven you twice this week..."*

Joey: *"Oh Mom... please?"*

Mom (letting out a big sigh): *"Oh, all right!"*

Her body language and speech say, *"Just look at the sacrifices I make for you. If you loved me more, you'd appreciate me more!"*

Indirect Aggression

These people are between assertive and obviously aggressive. They use subtle, underhanded methods to get their way, such as sabotage, sarcasm, the silent treatment, sulking, and gossip. We discussed these methods earlier.

Aggressive

Aggressive people have little respect for other people's needs and rights. Things go their way or not at all. They railroad, bulldoze, and shove their ideas and wishes on others using persistence, coercion and even threats. They differ from other manipulators because they're obvious. You know they're out to get you.

Passive-aggressive

These people have a pathological reaction to authority and those they perceive in positions of authority. They tend to blow up unexpectedly, keeping others off balance because their behaviour often doesn't follow the usual pattern. Normally a person shows signs of frustration before they blow up – passive-aggressive people do it *"out of the blue."* They gain the trust of others, and then stab them in the back. This causes the other person to use caution when dealing with them, but they can be so charming that they worm their way into obtaining our trust. Then they repeat their pattern. We must always expect the unexpected with these people and be on guard should they repeat their destructive behaviour.

How passive people feel about themselves

People who normally use passive behaviour likely feel:

o   Angry - *they* know others take advantage of them;

o   Frustrated - they seldom get their way;

o   Withdrawn - they believe nobody listens to them;

o   Insecure and inferior - they lack self-esteem and self-confidence, are unaware of their abilities, and are reluctant to try new things for fear of failing;

o   Anxious - they believe it's no use trying, they won't get what they want anyway;

o   Unable to acknowledge feelings - they hide feelings of fear and inadequacy by pretending everything's all right;

o Liable to put themselves down - they have difficulty accepting even the simplest compliment and tend to underestimate the value of what they do;

o Lacking in energy - their zest for life is missing. They're usually doing things that others want them to do, rather than what *they* themselves want.

These people believe they're not okay, but you are okay.

How aggressive people feel about themselves

People who normally use aggressive behaviour likely feel:

o Powerful (in the short run) - they enjoy having people scurry and rush to do what they say;

o Guilty (eventually) - they know they're taking advantage of others;

o Threatened - they constantly let others know how good, intelligent, strong, etc. they are.

o They do this because others may learn they aren't really that good underneath their veneer.

o They attempt to make themselves feel important by putting others down;

o Right - they are convinced that the only ideas worth listening to are their own;

o Critical - they blame others when things go wrong;

o Lonely - their aggression isolates them from everyone around them;

o Excessively energetic - they expend energy in the wrong direction, doing destructive rather than constructive things.

These people feel that they're okay, but you're not okay. Those who hit the outer edge of aggressive behaviour (criminals) believe that they're not okay, but you are not okay either.

How assertive people feel about themselves

People who normally use assertive behaviour likely feel:

o Positive - they approach every new task or idea with a positive, rather than a negative attitude;

o Calm - they're at peace with themselves and others;

o Enthusiastic - they complete tasks with zest and feel that they'll succeed at them;

o Proud - they accomplish what they do without stealing ideas from others or climbing over others. They can take full credit for what they achieve;

o Honest - when they give their word that they'll do something, they do it, so others believe in them;

o Direct - they don't play manipulative games to get what they want. They deal up-front in situations, and usually succeed at whatever they attempt;

o Confident - they take risks but know their limitations. They know that it's okay to be wrong sometimes and are ready to learn from their mistakes;

o Satisfied - they know where they're going and how they're going to get there, so they usually attain their goals;

o In control - they seldom have mood swings that adversely affect communication with, and behaviour towards others;

o Able to acknowledge feelings - they can explain to others what unpleasant behaviour is doing to them;

o Respect for others - they recognise that others have needs and rights just as they do;

o Energetic - their energy is directed towards achieving their goals.

These people feel that they're okay, and you're okay too.

Consequences of these behavioural styles

It's helpful to know how others are likely to react to you when you use different behavioural styles.

Passive behaviour

Passive behaviour can make others feel aggressive. People may shun someone who gives in again and again to their wishes.

They don't like the guilty feelings they have when passive people allow themselves to be taken advantage of.

For example, Sarah was responsible for ensuring that the receptionist in the office, Judy, had someone to take over her duties during coffee, lunch and bathroom breaks. There were four employees on the list that Sarah could call on for this duty. Several of them were sick or couldn't spare the time one week, so Mary had to cover for Judy all that week. This made Mary fall behind in her own work, and she had to work overtime two days that week.

The same problem existed the next two weeks, and Sarah had to rely on Mary again. Mary willingly worked the second week. Sarah felt terrible asking her to cover the post the third week, but grudgingly, Mary again agreed.

From then on, every time Sarah saw Mary, she felt guilty. She realised that, although she was normally an assertive person, she felt as though she had taken advantage of Mary (had acted aggressively) and she felt guilty. To combat this guilty feeling, she avoided Mary and didn't have normal contact with her.

Mary helped Sarah out because she wanted Sarah to like her but ended up with a negative reaction (exactly what she tried not to do). Many passive people have this unexpected reaction to their *"good deeds"* and wonder what they've done wrong and how they may have offended others.

Dealing with passive people can also make others feel:

- Irritated - they wish you'd stand up for yourself and make your own decisions;
- Withdrawn - they avoid you because your negative attitude makes it hard for them to maintain their positive attitude;
- Superior - they lose respect for you as a person, because you aren't willing to stand up for what you believe in;
- Tired - they waste valuable energy dealing with their negative reactions to you.

Aggressive behaviour

Aggressive behaviour can make others feel:

- Angry and threatened - they resent your unfair tactics;
- Frustrated - they waste valuable energy defending themselves from your abusive ways;
- Withdrawn - they avoid you because when you're around, they feel they must be ready to defend themselves;
- Anxious and defensive - they can't relax because they're preparing for the next attack;
- Resentful - they resent the power you seem to have over them;
- Hurt - they can't help being affected by your put-downs, even if they know your comments are undeserved;
- Humiliated - they don't enjoy being corrected or made to appear foolish in public;
- Tired - they waste valuable energy preparing for what you're going to throw at them next.

Assertive behaviour

Assertive behaviour can make others feel:

- Positive - they sense that you will be pleased if they succeed,
- Secure - they trust you, because you let them know where they stand with you by offering constant feedback;
- Cooperative - they respond to your straightforward positive behaviour by trying to help you;
- Respectful - they reciprocate the respect you show for their needs and rights;
- Energetic - they're able to use their energy constructively because there's no game playing.

Who wins?

Do assertive people achieve their goals? Yes, because their aim is for both sides to win. They believe in equality and are willing to negotiate.

Do passive people usually achieve their goals? No, because they seldom have goals in the first place. They expect others to look after them.

Do aggressive people usually achieve their goals? Sometimes, in the short run, but they often face antagonism and retaliation later.

You are now equipped with some basic insights into human behaviour - your own and that of others. You will be able to switch off your defence mechanism when faced with negative comments and actions from others. The tool that will allow you to make effective use of these insights is your ability to communicate well with the people you encounter.

CHAPTER FOUR
BASIC COMMUNICATION SKILLS

If you find that you're often misunderstood, or that you misunderstand others too often, the following skill is a must for you to practice and use.

Paraphrasing

Paraphrasing is to express meaning in other words; to rephrase; to give a message in another form; to amplify a message.

We normally use paraphrasing for such simple things as repeating telephone numbers when taking a message. If you simply repeat the person's message, that's parroting. If you ask yourself what the person means and ask for confirmation of your understanding of their message, that's paraphrasing. Of the two methods, paraphrasing is much more effective.

The use of paraphrasing is essential when two people are conversing at any time. Unfortunately, when information isn't clear to us, we often make assumptions. We don't confirm with other people that what we *thought* they said was what they really meant us to understand.

For example, you are receiving instructions on how to get to someone's house. You neglected to use paraphrasing to confirm that you have understood the directions, and you end up completely lost. Sound familiar?

Here's an example of two people talking but not understanding each other:

Bill: *"Jim didn't get that job he wanted."*

Jennie: *"He didn't get the job he wanted?"*

Bill: *"Yeah, and he's really upset about it."*

In this conversation, Jennie thought she was using paraphrasing, but all she was doing was parroting what Bill said. Instead, she should have asked herself what Bill's statement *meant* to her. Some of her assumptions could have been:

1. Jim asked for too much money.
2. He was over-qualified for the position.
3. He was under-qualified for the position.
4. He blew the interview.
5. Someone else was better than he.
6. He's probably better suited to a different career.

If she had determined what the statement meant to her (Jim blew the interview) and had used paraphrasing, the earlier conversation would have been more like this.

Bill: *"Jim didn't get the job he wanted."*

Jennie: *"You mean he blew the interview?"*

Bill: *"Oh no, he learned that they had already chosen someone else for the position before he applied."*

Jennie: *"I'm sorry to hear that."*

Bill: *"Yeah, and he's really upset about it."*

You can see the difference between these two sets of conversations. In the first conversation, Bill and Jennie do not confirm their personal beliefs with each other. Bill believes that Jennie knows Jim didn't get the job because they had someone else chosen for the position. Jennie, on the other hand, believes that Bill has confirmed her conviction that Jim blew the interview. Therefore, problems occurred later. In a conversation with another friend, Jennie stated that both she and Bill agreed that Jim had blown the interview. She honestly believed that she was speaking the truth to her friend.

This kind of problem arises in many conversations. Ask for more information if you're not sure what the person means or use paraphrasing to bring out discrepancies. You probably use this technique already but haven't been aware of it. If anyone has ever exclaimed, *"No, that's not what I meant,"* you've already used paraphrasing and maybe didn't even know it! Use it often; it lessens communication problems.

Paraphrasing is also an excellent tool to use when clients are angry at something. If you write down details of the situation you're trying to correct, you're less likely to be spending your energy defending yourself. When the client has given all the information you need to solve the problem, use paraphrasing to make sure s/he knows you understand. The client will likely calm down and give you the opportunity to help.

Using paraphrasing when training others

If you've had the responsibility of training others, you've probably had to explain more than once how to do something. Paraphrasing is a very effective tool to use when training others, especially if they are lazy listeners. To help them retain their training, do the following:

1. Give short, sequential instructions.

2. State, *"To make sure that I was clear in my instructions to you, could you please explain what you're going to do?"*

3. If the trainee is unable to recite the steps, repeat the instructions.

4. Again, ask the trainee to recite the steps s/he will take to complete the task.

You'll find that trainee's listening skills will improve immeasurably when you use this technique. They'll know that when you train them to do anything new, there'll be a test to see if they've listened properly, and you'll find that giving instructions will be much easier in the future.

Do, however, remember that the onus is on you to make your instructions clear. Avoid such questions as:

- *"Do you understand?"* (People can just answer yes to this. You want to double-check by having them repeat the instructions back to you.)

- *"Explain what I want you to do."* (This is too overbearing. It will just put people's backs up).

- *"Did you catch that?"* (This sounds like a put-down. People will resent the implication that they're stupid.)

If you think people might have misunderstood you, it's much better to make the problem yours. You can accomplish this by saying something like: *"Let's see if I've been clear in my instructions to you."* You could then ask if they have any questions.

Different interpretations of words

Many words mean different things to different people. For example, if I invited you to my home for dinner tomorrow, when would you come? Would it be at noon or one o'clock, or at five, six, seven or eight o'clock? Some people have *dinner* (the main meal of the day) at midday, others in the evening.

If I asked people from Queensland and Antarctica to describe a blizzard, do you think their descriptions would be the same? Of course, not - each person has a different experience of what this word means. (And a teenager might describe a blizzard as an ice cream treat that you eat!)

These following elements are all part of the communication process:

- What I want to say/think I'm saying.
- What I say.
- What others think they hear.
- What others want to reply/think they're replying.
- What others reply.
- What I think I hear them say.

Sensory Language

When we say two people have *"rapport"* we usually mean their relationship is harmonious - we connect with someone else's world. We can enhance this rapport by determining their primary sensory language.

People process information in different ways. They are primarily visual, auditory or kinaesthetic (muscular movement) in the way they process information. Most people are a mixture of all three, but one usually stands out as being their primary sensory language. Each type uses distinctive words that reflect their preference. To create rapport with people, listen to them to find out their primary mode, then mirror their language.

Here are examples within each type of primary sensory language:

The visual person might say:

"I get the picture."

"I see what you mean."

"Let me see what the job looks like." Or,

"My perception is..."

The auditory person uses such phrases as:

"That sounds good to me."

"I hear what you're saying."

"That rings a bell."

"I hear you loud and clear."

"She's not in tune with me." Or;

"Let me explain how this works."

Typical phrases for kinaesthetic would be:

"Show me how to do this."

"That doesn't feel right."

"Hold on."

"I'm comfortable with that."

"I'll give you a feel for the job."

"I grasp what you're saying."

"That's a rough problem." Or,

"You have a heavy task."

Now, do the following:

1. Determine your primary sensory language.

2. Determine the primary sensory language of the people you deal with.

3. What changes can you make to communicate on the wavelength of your difficult people?

Those who are responsible for training others have probably thrown their hands up in the air at times. Their information seems to go in one ear and out the other with some learners. Many people require constant repetition of instructions. This type of person may be a poor listener.

Information has a better chance of being "locked in" when trainers use a variety of training methods. These could include visual aids such as movies, slides or flip charts. To help trainees further "lock in" the training, they should use the training as soon as possible. Keep in mind that trainees retain:

- 10 per cent of what they read (handouts, manuals);

- 20 per cent of what they hear (have explained to them);

- 30 per cent of what they see done (demonstrations);

- 50 per cent of what they read, hear and see demonstrated;

- 70 per cent of what they read, hear, see demonstrated and explain to someone else;

- 90 per cent of what they read, hear, see demonstrated, explain to someone else and demonstrate themselves.

So, you can see that the more sensory language methods you use, the better the training is retained.

People pass through four definite stages when learning something new. These stages are:

1. *Unconscious incompetence* - They aren't even aware that they lack the skill. For example, they may not even have known that the skill of paraphrasing existed.

2. *Conscious incompetence* - They're aware that they lack the skill. For example, before they learned how to use a computer, they knew they couldn't use a computer.

3. *Conscious competence* - They know the techniques of the skill but need to stop and think before they react. (*"Do I put the disk in first or turn the computer on first?"*)

4. *Unconscious competence* - The skill is now well established and automatic. They probably don't even think about what they're doing when they use the computer - they're on *"automatic pilot."*

It takes six weeks to *"lock in"* how to do something new, and up to three months to *"lock in"* doing something a different way than you used to.

Male and Female Interpretations

Unfortunately, the simple act of communicating with one another can cause confused messages, or messages being missed entirely. This is especially true when it comes to communication between men and women. It's no wonder there's conflict, when they interpret the same conversation in different ways. This is because of the different conversational styles of men and women.

Many examples will stereotype male and female responses. There are many exceptions to the situations I've identified. Analyse how you feel or respond to situations; compare them to those described and decide if you need to change anything in your communication style.

As women grow up, talk is the thread from which relationships are woven. They develop and maintain friendships by exchanging secrets, and regard talking as the cornerstone of friendships. Men bond as intensely as women, but their friendships are based more on doing things together and don't require talk to cement relationships. Men converse to negotiate status; women to create rapport. Men are comfortable telling people what to do; women don't like to pull rank, so request rather than demand (which leads the man to believe they have the right to accept or refuse the woman's request).

When conversing, women face each other directly with eyes anchored on each other's faces. Men sit at angles to each other and look elsewhere in the room, periodically glancing at each other and often mirror each other's body movements. Men's tendency to face away from them when conversing, gives women the impression that the men aren't listening to them, when in fact they are. The only times men will really look for any time at the person who's speaking are:

- When they're trying to evaluate whether the speaker is lying or not;

- The person is hostile, and they may have to take defensive action; or,

- They're evaluating an attractive woman.

In the latter, they'll glance over the woman's body while listening to her comments. This is highly distracting to the female speaker because his eyes mirror that he's not really listening to what she's saying, but rather sizing her up as a woman.

Another habit that gives women the impression men aren't listening is that they switch topics more often. Women tend to talk at length about one topic - men tend to jump from topic to topic. When a woman expresses her point of view, her female listener usually expresses agreement and support, whereas men point out the other side of the issue. Women see this as disloyalty and a refusal to offer support to their ideas. Women prefer other points of view expressed as suggestions and enquiries rather than as direct challenges or arguments. Men are more comfortable with an oppositional style.

Men expect silent attention and interpret constant listener noise as signs of impatience on the listener's part. When men don't make listening noises, women may assume they're not listening to them. Women make more listening noises like *"un-huh..."* to encourage the other person. Men often believe these noises mean the woman agrees with him, when she may not agree with him at all. Because men don't make as many listening noises, women assume they're not really listening. Men are less likely to make non-verbal signs of listening as well, and many continue doing whatever they were doing before the conversation began. Women are more likely to nod their head more, give direct eye contact, and stop whatever else they may have been doing when the conversation began.

Women often overlap and finish each other's sentences (normally, neither is offended). Men clam up or react defensively when women do this to them, because they feel the woman's trying to take over the conversation. Men feel it's rude to finish another's comments and shows lack of attention to what they're saying, but, on the other hand, they are more likely to interrupt a speaker with negative side comments.

Feedback

Feedback is useful in both positive and negative contexts. Examples of positive feedback might include giving recognition for a job well done or paying someone a sincere compliment. In this section, we'll be concentrating on the uses of feedback in dealing with negative or difficult situations.

Use feedback if you've been upset or annoyed by something someone has done. You identify what they're doing that bothers you and give them the opportunity to do something about it. We're being unfair to others when we don't communicate these issues to them.

Consider the following series of events:

- When a person does something that bothers you, a small blip occurs on your *"screen of annoyance"*. Because it's only a small blip you decide to say nothing.

- The person does something else that annoys you, and another, bigger blip occurs on your screen of annoyance.

- The blips soon accumulate, and you have a major blow-up with the person.

The most trivial final incident can trigger this response. How much better it would have been to handle each blip immediately and keep it from being recorded on your screen of annoyance.

There are many different situations when it is appropriate to use the feedback process. For example, you should let others know when you:

- Don't understand what they've said;

- Like something they've said or done;

- Disagree with them;

- Think they've changed the subject or are going around in circles;

- Are becoming annoyed;

- Feel hurt or embarrassed.

Feedback also helps you keep in touch with your reactions, so you can deal with them before they turn into serious negative feelings of frustration, anger, hurt, defeat, fear, depression, dependence, weakness or defencelessness.

Most women are comfortable saying that they have such feelings, but men have been socialized to believe it's a weakness to acknowledge them. This limits their options for expressing their feelings. Many respond as if they're angry - an acceptable reaction among men – when they may feel hurt, or defenceless or afraid. Their ambiguous behaviour confuses women and widens the communication gap between men and women.

When a man appears upset, often a woman will ask, *"What's wrong?"* The man's response is often, *"Nothing,"* or, *"I don't want to talk about it."* This makes the woman feel as though she's shut out or rejected. This communication gap will be reduced if men stop and analyse what they're really feeling before they react.

Be selective when you use feedback. Always ask yourself first, *"Am I overreacting? Is my reaction unfair or petty?"* Feedback must be immediate and specific - don't save up grievances and don't dump too many things on a person at once. As well, there must be something the recipient of the feedback can do about the problem.

To be effective, there must also be a foundation of trust between the sender and receiver of the feedback. Otherwise, the feedback could be misinterpreted as a personal attack. The recipient may hear only the critical things and react defensively rather than listen to what you have to say.

Here are some general guidelines for giving feedback:

1. *Be sure the receiver is ready.* Give the feedback only when there are clear indications that the receiver is ready to listen to it. If not, the receiver won't hear it or is likely to misinterpret your comments.

2. ***Base your comments on facts, not emotions.*** Giving feedback acts like a *"candid camera."* It's a report of the facts, rather than your ideas about why things happened or what the person meant by them.

3. ***Be specific.*** Give quotes and examples of exactly what you're referring to.

4. ***Give feedback as soon after the event as possible.*** The closer you give feedback to the time the event took place, the better. If you give feedback immediately, the receiver is more likely to understand exactly what's meant. The feelings accompanying the event still exist, so this, too, can help.

5. ***Pick a convenient time.*** Feedback is given when there's a good chance the person will listen to it. It may not be helpful if the receiver feels there are already other matters that demand his/her attention.

6. ***Pick a private place.*** Critical feedback given in front of others will be damaging rather than helpful and is a form of bullying.

7. ***Concentrate on what can be changed.*** Feedback should be about things that can be changed should the receiver choose to do so.

8. ***Request cooperation.*** The receiver can consider whether s/he wishes to attempt a change based on your feedback information. You may wish to include that you would like to see certain changes. You're not likely to be successful if you give the impression of saying, *"I've told you what's wrong with you, now change!"*

9. ***Focus on one thing at a time.*** When learning how to give feedback, we may sometimes overdo it. It's as though we were telling the receiver, *"I just happen to have a list of reactions here. Let me read them off to you."* The receiver would naturally prefer time to consider each item and may baulk at your overwhelming expectations.

10. ***Be helpful.*** Always consider your own motives for giving your opinions. Are you trying to be helpful to the receiver

or are you unloading some of your own feelings? Are you using the occasion to try to get the receiver to do something that benefits only you? For example, if you're angry and wish to express it, say so – but include a description of the behaviour that caused your anger.

11. ***Encourage the recipient to provide feedback in return***. Giving feedback can become *"one-upmanship."* Because the giver has focused on the person's potential for improvement, the receiver goes away feeling as though s/he is *"not as good."* The exchange will be better balanced if the receiver has a chance to include some of his or her own feelings and concerns.

Here are some guidelines for receiving feedback:

1. ***State what you want feedback about.*** Help the giver provide useful reactions by asking for feedback about specific things.

2. ***Check what you've heard.*** Use paraphrasing to be sure you understand the giver's message.

3. ***Share your reactions to the feedback.*** As your own feelings become involved, you may forget to share your reactions to the feedback you've received. Knowing what was and was not helpful assists the giver to improve his or her ability to provide useful feedback. If the giver is uncertain about your reactions, s/he may be less apt to risk sharing in the future.

Here is an example of how to use feedback:

A receptionist had a problem she didn't know how to handle. She would take messages for all the office staff. One client (George Samuels) phoned in repeatedly, asking to speak to her supervisor. She promptly passed on his messages. The fourth time he called, the client accused her of not passing on his messages to her boss. She wondered how she should deal with this situation as it was likely going to happen again. What would you suggest she tell George Samuels the next time he phoned?

Did you notice that she was trying to deal with the wrong problem? Her supervisor was the problem, not the client. When I asked her if she had ever considered talking to her supervisor about the problem, she replied, *"Oh, I couldn't do that!"*

I then asked, *"How is the situation going to change unless he knows what his behaviour does to you? You're not even giving him the opportunity of solving this dilemma."*

There are three steps in the process of feedback.

Process of feedback

a) Describe the problem or situation to the person causing the difficulty.

b) Define what feelings or reactions (anger, sadness, anxiety, hurt, or distress) the problem behaviour causes you.

c) Suggest a solution or ask the person to provide a solution.

In the receptionist's case, she might have felt like saying, *"You idiot, you never return your telephone messages!"* But this kind of accusation would only get her supervisor's back up. Instead, she should try to gain his cooperation in solving the problem. She should say, *"I have a problem and I need your help in solving it. This client phoned in four times, and he's really annoyed at me because you haven't returned his calls. This upsets me. What do you suggest I tell him the next time he calls?"*

In this transaction, the following feedback steps were taken:

a) **The problem** - he's not returning his phone calls.

b) **Her feelings or reactions** - *"This upsets me."*

c) **The solution** - she asks her supervisor to provide one.

Here's another example:

Margo, a co-worker, is always interrupting you with small talk, which interferes with your concentration. You're getting annoyed with her. Your first reaction might be to blast her with a statement such as *"Margo, will you shut up and let me get my work done!"* Use feedback instead and say, *"Margot, I'm working on an important project. I'm sure you're not aware of this, but every time you interrupt me, I lose my train of thought. Can we talk later at coffee break?"*

a) **The problem** - she's interrupting your work.

b) **Her feelings or reactions** - you lose your train of thought.

c) **The solution** - you suggest talking later at coffee break.

Suppose Margo interrupts you again a couple of hours later. What should you tell her? (Remember, this might be a habit with Margo, and she may have done it without thinking.) What should your response be?

Repeat your original comments: *"As I mentioned earlier, I'm working on an important project. Every time you interrupt me, I lose my train of thought. Can we talk later at coffee break?"*

The next morning, guess what has happened? She's at it again. What should you do now? Many would suggest that you ignore her comments.

Instead you should say, *"Margo, twice yesterday I mentioned that I'm working on an important project and your interruptions affected my concentration. Can you tell me why you're still doing this?"*

What you're doing is making Margo account for her aggressive actions. (Yes, she's being aggressive, because she now *knows* she's bothering you).

Explain that if it happens again, you'll have to speak to Jim, your supervisor. This is the step most people miss. It explains clearly the consequences Margo will face if she does it again. Margo promises she won't do it again.

Another day goes by, and Margo's at it again! What should you do the fourth time? Don't just say you're going to do something - follow through and talk to your supervisor. Rather than giving the impression that you're going to *"tattle"* on your co-worker, ask for your supervisor's advice. Say, *"Jim, I have a problem and I need your help in solving it. On Tuesday, I spoke to Margo and asked her to..."*

Explain everything you've done up to this point to stop her negative behaviour. Then ask, *"What do you suggest I do next time she interrupts me?"*

Normally, he will talk to Margo himself, because Margo is wasting his department's budget and, ultimately, company money. As Margo reports to Jim, he is ultimately responsible for what she does – and she's making him look bad.

You might ask yourself, *"Will Margo like me after I've spoken to my supervisor?"* Who cares? She's going to cause you trouble whether you go to your supervisor or not.

Use the wording, *"I have a problem and need your help in solving it,"* whenever someone is causing you grief. This is especially effective if used on the person who is causing the problem! You're not shaking your finger at them and telling them off for their behaviour. You're asking their help in trying to solve it. Who should have been on top of the Margo situation? Her supervisor should have been. What you have done is dumped the problem that he should have handled in his lap - but you've done it in such a nice way that he'll feel obliged to solve it.

This approach often gets the results you're after when other approaches fail. Use this feedback technique whenever a person's pen-clicking, gum-chewing, chair-squeaking or loud voice affects your performance at work. Use it when people are late with their reports, or when their actions keep you from doing your job correctly.

To recap the follow-up steps in the process of feedback:

Feedback Steps

1. Follow a), b) and c) steps from the Process of Feedback.
   a. Describe the problem or situation to the person causing the difficulty.
   b. Define what feelings or reactions the problem behaviour causes you.
   c. Suggest a solution or ask the person to provide a solution.
2. Repeat #1.

3. a. Ask the person to explain why s/he's still doing something that s/he knows annoys you.

   b. Explain the consequences should the behaviour or situation happens again.

4. Follow through with the consequences.

Go directly to step 3 if faced with a person who refuses to cooperate.

Using Feedback with very difficult people

Among the wide range of human types, there are always a few people who are more difficult to deal with than others. A very difficult person isn't just someone who is having a bad day or with whom you have a personality conflict. A very difficult person is difficult often and with most people.

You *can* use feedback effectively for dealing with such people. However, because the risks that your attempt will backfire are greater, you will need to prepare extra carefully before you approach them.

Thorough advanced preparation is especially valuable when you're having problems with those in a position of power, such as your supervisor, a parent or an older person.

1. ***Determine the problem.*** Identify the specific behaviour that's unacceptable; who is affected by the behaviour; and how frequently it occurs. Concentrate on behaviour the person can do something about. If the problem occurs only with one person, it's most likely a personality conflict rather than difficult behaviour.

2. ***Examine relationships.*** Clues to the possible causes of the negative behaviour will be found by examining how the difficult person interacts with others around them. Determining why the behaviour occurs and why it's annoying you will help find solutions.

3. ***Determine the cost of the problem behaviour.*** Whether it's lost productivity, general discomfort or lower morale, difficult behaviour always carries a cost. The behaviour should be ignored if you can't determine any costs.

4. ***Prepare for the confrontation.*** Should you have determined that the costs are too high, it's now time to speak to the offender. What special concerns do you have about the problem? What difficulties might you experience in the discussion? How will you handle these problems? Be ready for most situations you may face. Determine what you want to accomplish, then set up a meeting where you'll have privacy and enough time to discuss the situation.

5. ***Rehearse thoroughly.*** Rehearse the trying situation beforehand with a friend. Your friend should have as much knowledge of the situation as possible. This way, s/he can formulate good arguments and be able to anticipate what the other person's objections or reactions might be. The adage that practice makes perfect works here. Remember that the person you're eventually going to deal with has not had the opportunity to practise.

6. ***Find a solution.*** In a non-accusatory manner, explain why the problem concerns you. Give specific facts. Try not to offer your opinion as to why the problem exists. Ask questions to check your understanding. Identify the change in behaviour you're seeking. Be open to changing your solution if it's inappropriate. Listen to the difficult person's ideas about how s/he can solve the problem. Express confidence in the person's ability to change.

7. ***Agree on a plan of action.*** Work towards a solution acceptable to both parties.

8. ***Obtain a commitment.*** Get agreement on specific actions the person will take and set a deadline for these actions. Ask the person to confirm that s/he will do what's been agreed upon.

9. ***Follow up with the person.*** Recognise and comment on any progress you've observed. Re-evaluate the action plan and revise it if necessary. If there's been no change, repeat the process.

Coping Strategy

One solution may be to make the best of a bad situation. You can minimise the damage caused by the difficult behaviour by:

- remaining calm - don't argue with the other person or make accusations;

- using your listening skills to check your understanding;

- being firm - decide in advance what behaviour you will or will not accept, and don't let yourself be pushed beyond this limit;

- being persistent and consistent in your response, which conveys to the difficult person that you mean what you say;

- believing in yourself and your ability to deal with others;

- looking for ways to lessen your exposure to the behaviour, or to reduce the causes of the behaviour.

Listening

We spend up to 80 per cent of our conscious hours using four basic communication skills; writing, reading, speaking and listening. Listening accounts for more than 50 per cent of that time, so we spend 40 per cent of our waking time just listening!

We listen in spurts. Most of us are unable to give hard, close attention to what others say for more than sixty seconds at a time. We concentrate for a while, our attention lags, then we concentrate again.

Have you ever received specific training on how to listen? Probably not. It was always, *"Patti, will you stop talking..."* not, *"Patti, will you please listen"* and give you the techniques you'd need to improve your listening skills.

How fast do you think the average person speaks in words per minute? (Keep in mind that secretaries usually take shorthand at 80 to 120 w.p.m. and court stenographers at 220 w.p.m.)

Normal speaking speed is 125 to 150 w.p.m. My speaking speed is at least 160 w.p.m. especially when I'm conducting seminars. This bothered me at one time.

What do you think your thinking capability is in w.p.m.? I've heard guesstimates from 50 to 300 w.p.m. The average person can think at the phenomenal speed of 750 to 1,200 w.p.m.!

Then why don't we hear what people tell us? Because our minds are bored, that's why. There's not enough happening to keep our brains occupied when people speak at normal speeds. Even my speaking speed of 160 w.p.m. can't always keep participants motivated during a seminar all the time. So, what happens? We all go on side-trips (tune-outs) where we may start finding examples of something the person's discussing, wonder why our spouse was in such a bad mood that morning, admire something someone is wearing and wonder where they bought it, or wonder if it's time for a coffee break

Radio and television have turned most of us into lazy listeners. For instance, did you turn the radio on this morning to catch the weather forecast or the news? Did you hear it? Or did you tune out the voices and miss it entirely? It takes practice and concentration to stay tuned in to what's being said.

Kinds of bad listeners

There are several problem listeners that we all need to deal with. Here are a few:

- **Bashful people.** Because shy people expect others to draw them out, they place emotional demands on everyone they're with. If they don't receive this attention, they tune out. Most shy people aren't aware of this negative behaviour, nor of the demands it places on others around them.

- **Anxious people.** Because they lack confidence, they are nervous chatterers. They worry about what *they're* going to say next, which leaves little room for listening to others.

- **Argumentative people.** They'd argue with Einstein about his theory of relativity! They nitpick small details, which breaks conversational flow.

- **Opinionated people.** These people spend their energy formulating their own arguments, rather than listening to others. They interrupt and begin every other sentence with, *"But..."* Such people may be overly anxious to impress others, but they often produce the opposite effect. People tune them out.

- *Closed-minded people.* The most infuriating of bad listeners, they have rigid sets of values and find security in their prejudices. Any new ideas or changes leave them feeling threatened.

When faced with these poor listeners, use feedback to explain how you feel. Use of tact and empathy will assist you in helping them to become better listeners. Explain to closed-minded people that they've literally shut you out, that their unwillingness to listen to your ideas makes you feel rejected and unimportant. If you explain this, and the person continues to behave in the same way, you can (a) put up with it, or (b) use steps 2 to 4 of the feedback process.

Most poor listeners aren't aware of their failings. Your feedback may be helpful in changing their attitude and behaviour.

Blocks to effective listening

There are other things that can lead you astray when listening. Ask yourself which ones cause you problems:

- You had trouble understanding the speaker's words or lacked the knowledge to gasp the message (The speaker was using unfamiliar language, jargon or technical terms.)

- You were thinking of what you were going to say while the speaker was talking.

- You were preoccupied with how strongly you disagreed with the speaker's views.

- You listened for what you wanted to hear.

- You were too tired mentally to work at paying attention.

- There were outside noises and distractions.

- The speaker had poor delivery - slow, windy, irrelevant, rambling, or repetitious.

- Something the speaker said intrigued you; you thought about it, and when you *"tuned back in"* you'd lost the thread of the conversation.

- The speaker had an accent and you had difficulty understanding

- You tuned out because you thought you knew what the speaker's conclusions were going to be.

- You forgot to use paraphrasing and feedback in listening effectively

- You felt you were being given far too much information

How do you rate as a listener?

Rate yourself (or have a friend help you) using the following scale:

5= Always
4= Almost always
3= Sometimes
2= Rarely
1= Never

1. I allow the speaker to express his or her complete thoughts without interrupting.

2. I actively try to develop my ability to remember important facts.

3. In a conference or important phone conversation, I write down the most important details of a message.

4. I avoid becoming hostile or excited if a speaker's views differ from mine.

5. I repeat the essential details of a conversation back to the speaker to confirm that I have understood correctly.

6. I exercise tact in keeping the speaker on track.

7. I tune out distractions when listening.

8. I try to show interest in the other person's conversation.

9. I understand that I'm learning little when I'm talking. (I talk too much, listen too little?)

10. I sound as if I'm listening. (I use paraphrasing, ask questions.)

11. I remember that people are less defensive when they feel they're being understood.

12. I understand that I don't have to agree with the speaker.

13. In personal conversation, I look for non-verbal forms of communication, such as body language, tone of voice and other signals that provide information in addition to the speaker's words.

14. I look as if I'm listening in personal meetings. (I lean forward, give eye contact.)

15. I ask for the spelling of names and places when I'm taking a message

Total:

Scoring:

> 64 or more - You're an excellent listener!
> 50 – 63 - You're better than average.
> 40 – 49 - You require improvement.
> 39 or less - You're not an effective listener. You need practice, practice and more practice!

To elaborate on question 12: Suppose, in a conversation with someone about a controversial topic (such as abortion or capital punishment) you discover the two of you are on opposite sides of the issue. If your discussion is going nowhere but is making both of you angry, use the *agree to disagree* procedure.

To elaborate on question 15: When you're taking down people's names, ask them to confirm the spelling (even the name Smith may be spelled Smythe). In brackets (below the spelling of the name) add your own phonetic pronunciation of the name. For instance, the last name Tozer would be phonetically *Toe-zer;* Blecha - *Blek-ka;* Carphin - *Car-fin;* Cebuliak - *Seb-u-luck.*

This technique is very helpful to the person who will be returning the call. I use it on client files, so that I can pronounce the person's name properly when I contact him or her in the future.

How to improve your listening skills

1. You must care enough to want to improve. Without this motivation, it'll be too much effort.

2. Try to find an uninterrupted area in which to converse. Keeping your train of thought is difficult when there are obstructions to concentration.

3. Try not to anticipate what the other person will say.

4. Be mindful of your own biases and prejudices, so they don't unduly influence your listening.

5. Pay careful attention to what's being said. Don't stop listening so you can plan a rebuttal to a point.

6. Be aware of *"red flag"* words that might trigger an overreaction or a stereotypical reaction. Examples of this are *"women's libber"* or *"male chauvinist."*

7. Don't allow yourself to get too far ahead of the speaker by trying to understand things too soon.

8. At intervals, try to paraphrase what people are saying. Give them the opportunity to learn what you think you've heard them say.

9. When you have difficulty determining the point of the speaker's remarks, say, *"Why are you telling me this?"*

10. Watch for key or buzz words if you find you've lost the train of the conversation. This happens particularly when the speaker is long-winded or tends to ramble.

11. Don't interrupt to demand clarification of insignificant or irrelevant details.

Qualities of a good listener

People who practise good listening skills do the following:

1. Let others finish what they're saying without interrupting them.

2. Ask questions if they're confused.

3. Pay attention to what others are saying and show they're paying attention by keeping comfortable eye contact. They don't let their eyes wander around the room.

4. Remain open-minded, ready to revise their opinion.

5. Use feedback and paraphrasing skills.

6. Pay attention to non-verbal signals such as body language.

7. Don't tune out inappropriately when others are speaking.

Speaking

Another communication skill is the art of being able to say what you want to say, when you want to say it. Verbal fluency enables you to express your thoughts clearly, so others understand exactly what you mean. Here is a test you can give yourself. As we often don't see ourselves clearly, it might be a benefit to have a friend do it for you as well.

How do you rate as a speaker?

Rate yourself (or have a friend help you) using the following scale:

5= Always
4= Almost always
3= Sometimes
2= Rarely
1= Never

1. If I were a listener, would I listen to myself?

2. If I'm being misunderstood, I remember that it's my responsibility to help the other person understand me.

3. I keep my instructions to others short, sweet and to the point.

4. I am aware of when my audience has tuned me out.

5. I make sure my listeners know what I want from them.

6. When I give instructions, I ask for feedback and paraphrasing to make sure I'm understood.

7. I make sure my non-verbal signals (body language, tone of voice, etc.) are the same as my verbal ones.

8. I make sure I don't intimidate my listeners with a loud voice, threatening appearance, intense or prolonged eye contact, verbal attacks, etc.

9. I articulate clearly.

10. I try to use language the listener can understand.

Total:

Scoring:

> 40 or more - You're an excellent speaker!
> 32 – 39 - You're better than average.
> 25 – 31 - You require improvement.
> 24 or less- You're not an effective speaker. You need practice, practice and more practice!

Did you chuckle to yourself when responding to the first question? Did you find there was an element of truth in it? It's possible that you are one of those people who believe they're not worth listening to. There are three main reasons why you may feel you're not a good speaker.

1. ***You have trouble getting the words out.*** Some people know what they want to say but can't quite say it. (They lack verbal fluency.) You could try joining Toastmaster or Toastmistress clubs or take a public-speaking course. Because you're going to be talking the rest of your life, it certainly seems worthwhile to improve this essential communication skill.

2. ***You're not up on what's going on.*** Often people insulate themselves from anything outside their own little world. Then, in social situations, they find they're not up on current events and have nothing to contribute to the conversation. The solution is to catch up on what's happening.

3. ***You're a motor mouth.*** Some people have problems keeping conversations short, sweet and to the point. Take the time to organize your thoughts before you speak. Practise by writing down your thoughts or use a tape recorder. Then reword your remarks, using more precise language.

The suggestions in point 3 will also be useful if you have trouble giving clear instructions. Use the KISS principle: Keep It Simple, Sweetie (or Keep It Simple, Stupid - depending on how you feel at the time).

To ensure that your listeners know what you want from them, ask them for their help before you give them the background information.

For example, a man wanted to discuss a work problem with his wife, who had just put in a rather tiring day herself. He proceeded to give her all kinds of details about what was happening. When he asked, *"What do you think I should do?"* she was embarrassed, because she had been only half-listening. He had to tell her all the details again before she could answer. It would have been so much better if he had started out the conversation, *"Victoria, I need your opinion on something that's happening at the office. Do you have time to discuss it right now?"* Then he would have confirmed that she did have time, and she would have been aware that he needed her undivided attention.

Avoiding ambiguous messages

Sometimes our words and behaviour are open to more than one interpretation. If we don't realize this and clarify our intended meaning, our behaviour can be misinterpreted. Here's an example:

1. ***Supervisor's intention.*** A supervisor wants to let Mary (one of his staff) know that he recognizes and appreciates the extra load she's been carrying lately. He debates which of the following would be best to communicate his appreciation:

   a. Giving Mary some time off;
   b. Taking Mary out to lunch;
   c. Telling Mary how he feels;
   d. Trying to reduce Mary's workload.

2. ***Supervisor's action.*** He decides on (d) and eases up on Mary's workload.

3. **Mary's reaction.** Mary notices the reduced workload but doesn't know what it means. Her supervisor might be:
   a. Criticising her for not having kept up with her workload;
   b. Trying to tell her she shouldn't spend so much time on the phone;
   c. Trying to be helpful;
   d. Convinced she can't handle crisis situations.

4. **Effect on Mary.** She decides it's (a) and feels hurt and put down.

5. **Mary encodes:** *"I'm not going to let him know that he's hurt me. Shall I:"*
   a. Say nothing?
   b. Say, *"thanks?"*

6. **Mary's action.** She decides to say *"Thanks."*

7. **Effect on supervisor.** He believes that Mary understands and appreciates what he's done.

The above situation is a classic example of how ambiguous behaviour can be misunderstood. The supervisor's intention was positive and caring. However, the effect on his employee was the direct opposite of what he wanted. It would have been much better if he had backed his actions up with words. By using positive feedback, he would have made sure Mary knew why he was easing her workload.

The following example illustrates the sometimes-serious consequences that can result from failure to explain ambiguous behaviour. A company was doing well, even though the economy was down. The company had decided to move its facilities to a larger, more comfortable building. The good news was to be announced to employees at a meeting planned for 5:00 p.m. Thursday. The problems began when workers from another company came to the reception desk Monday morning. They told the receptionist they were there to measure the offices. Asked why, they explained, *"Because the new owners need this information before they move in."*

After checking with her office manager, the receptionist gave permission to the workers to measure the offices. She began having the awful feeling that she might be out of a job soon. During coffee break, she mentioned the situation to two other co-workers, who of course passed this information on to others. By Tuesday afternoon, word reached the company executives that half their staff was applying for jobs with other companies because they believed that Thursday's meeting would announce the folding of their company. Management quickly decided to announce the good news on Tuesday at 5:00 p.m.

Understanding non-verbal signals

You notice that a friend you're having lunch with has some food on the corner of her mouth. You want to bring this to her attention in a tactful way. You take your napkin and wipe your own face, but at the same time look at your friend's face where the food is. In many cases she will wipe her face too, although she wouldn't be able to explain why she did so.

We *"hear"* what people say partly through what their body language, tone of voice, etc., tell us. Being able to interpret non-verbal signals is probably one of the best assets anyone can have. If you want to be a good communicator, it's essential to be aware of and try to understand such non-verbal signals. The only people who can lie consistently without having their body language give them away, are con artists and compulsive liars. This is because, they believe the lies they're telling. Here are some examples of what body language can tell us:

- *Tapping fingers.* The person is annoyed, impatient or anxious.

- *Shifting weight from one foot to another.* The person has been standing too long or is impatient.

- *Frowning.* The person doesn't understand what's being said or disagrees with what's being said.

- *Flushed face.* The person is embarrassed, angry or hot, or has high blood pressure. You'd have to look for other non-verbal signs to confirm which one it was.

- *Clenched jaw.* The person is upset, angry or anxious. This signal is more obvious in men than women.

- *Hand cupped around ear.* The person didn't hear what you said.

- *Slumped posture.* The person is tired, relaxed or depressed.

- *Avoidance of eye contact.* The person is shy, or bored. Or the person is from another culture that regards eye contact with the elderly or those in positions of authority as disrespectful. This signal is often misinterpreted as a sign of shifty behaviour or lack of self-confidence, when the cause may be something quite different.

- *Rapid or abrupt speech.* The person is upset, worried, anxious or angry.

- *Rise in voice volume.* The person is nervous or angry.

- *Rise in voice pitch.* A sign in women that the person is nervous or angry.

- *Drop in voice pitch.* A sign in men that the person is nervous or angry.

- *Jumpy body movements.* The person is nervous, anxious or angry.

- *Nose-scratching.* The person is puzzled or dislikes something. Or the person's nose may be itchy.

- *Shrugging.* The person is indifferent or doesn't know the answer.

- *Forehead-slapping.* The person feels forgetful or stupid.

- *Arms across chest.* The person feels defensive, physically cold or physically awkward. This may frequently be seen when men sit in chairs without arms, or simply because it's comfortable to do so.

- *Back-slapping.* The person is offering congratulations, or perhaps encouragement.

- *Clasping both hands over the head.* The person feels triumphant, pleased, and successful.

- *Holding the hand up, palm outwards.* This means *"Stop!"*

- *Thumb-and-finger-circling.* The person is saying *"Okay,"* or, *"Right!"* In some cultures, this is seen as an obscene gesture.

- *Poking you in the ribs.* The person is sharing a joke or teasing you.

We often place our hand on the arm or shoulder of an upset person. With close friends, relatives, children or elderly persons we might put an arm around their shoulder or hug them to give comfort.

We shake hands with people, an important non-verbal exchange. Originally, this communication meant that we were extending our empty weapon hand to show that we came as a friend. Now it can mean that we are giving our word that the exchange to follow is above board; that we are trustworthy. Women in business should practise until they feel comfortable giving a firm handshake. At a job interview, candidates should offer their hand first, rather than wait for the interviewer to do so. This indicates a high degree of self-confidence in a way that's hard to duplicate.

When you're interested in what others are saying, you might lean forward. You might also lean forward when you wish to speak next.

When people feel they are in a position of power, they often show dominance by deliberately interrupting others. They stand with feet straddled, hands on hips (a parental stance). They may fail to step aside when on a collision course with others. They may hold eye contact longer than is comfortable for the recipient, or hover or lean over others while watching them work. (If someone does this to you, stop working and use the feedback technique to explain what his or her behaviour is doing to you.)

Men who want to show their power will straddle a chair. Others will put their feet up on a desk and ostentatiously not remove them when someone comes into the room.

Power-hungry people take up more space on couches or benches than is their due. Don't encourage people to do this at the expense of others. Do something!

I remember one time when I had been travelling all day and was bone tired. There was a one-hour wait between connections at an airport. The place was crowded with travellers. I spotted a man sitting at one end of a bench. Taking up the rest of the bench were his briefcase, suitcase and overcoat.

I approached him and asked, *"Is this your briefcase?"* He nodded. I removed the briefcase from the bench and placed it in front of him.

"Is this your suitcase?" He nodded. I removed the suitcase from the bench and placed it in front of him.

Before I could ask him, *"Is this your overcoat?"* he removed it and placed it on his lap. I smiled and sat down right next to him.

Shortly after, two other tired travellers joined us on the bench. Their body language and smiles thanked me for the effort I had made.

People who lack assurance show this by their body language as well. Their posture shows defeat, there's little eye contact, and their voices are soft. They take up as little space as possible (pull all their *"ends"* in) or wear a fixed smile.

People who are lying may give themselves away through non-verbal signals. When people are being open with you, their body language usually indicates openness. They show their hands openly, for example. When they are hiding something, their body language changes. They may hide their hands in their pockets or behind their backs. If you accuse them of something, they'll likely give you an incredulous look and reply, *"Who me?"* They may put their hand on their chest (a non-verbal sign of honesty).

Note: The hand-to-the-chest gesture when used by women may also be a protective gesture showing sudden surprise or shock), but other body language may contradict this. Look for signals that identify a person who is lying by such behaviours as:

- Avoiding eye contact (usually by looking down);
- Blinking rapidly;
- Twitching and swallowing repeatedly;
- Clearing the throat and wetting the lips often;
- Covering the mouth with hand when speaking;
- Shrugging;
- Rubbing the nose;
- Scratching the head while talking;
- Putting a hand on the throat;
- Rubbing the back of the neck (a sure sign men are lying).

Space Bubbles

We all have a *"space bubble"* of safety around us - a gap between us and others that we need to maintain to feel secure. For most people, this bubble extends about eighteen to twenty-four inches (forty to sixty centimetres) from their bodies.

There are several types of distances we normally keep between others and ourselves. These are:

- **Intimate distance.** Only people we trust are welcome within our space bubble. We welcome people who are near and dear to us into this space, but we often need to endure others as well. This can be at the theatre, on a bus, at a seminar or in an elevator. You can probably think of hundreds of instances where we need to tolerate this closeness.

  Watch yourself when you're in an elevator. You naturally pull in all your *"ends"* and take up as little space as possible. Should you inadvertently touch the stranger next to you, you'll automatically say, *"Oops, I'm sorry,"* and pull away. This would also happen if you touched someone in a bank line-up or at a checkout counter.

- **Personal distance** is the space you usually keep with others when you have enough room to be comfortable. This is anywhere between three and four feet (one and one-and-a-half metres), depending on your comfort zone and how well you know the person. In elevators, as soon as the crowd thins, people will automatically widen the space between themselves and others.

- **Social distance** is four to seven feet (one-and-a-half to two metres). Strangers or acquaintances sitting on chairs or couches at a party will try to maintain this distance.

- **Far social distance.** This could happen at a large party or be the distance between a speaker and his or her audience.

Territorial supremacy

Not only do we try to keep a certain quantity of space around us, but also, we try to retain physical control over anything we think belongs to us. This may be a desk at work; our bedroom, kitchen or workshop; our car or boat; or our brush and comb. Others may use these articles only when we've given them permission to do so. That is why we may react violently when someone takes something of ours without permission.

The office receptionist is often the victim of *"territorial invasions."* Other office workers somehow think that it's okay to help themselves to the bottle of whiteout or the stapler on her desk. They may even open her desk drawers and help themselves to her scissors or ruler. Try to remember that the desk is *hers*. Don't take anything that you haven't asked permission to use. Should *you* be the receptionist, designate a communal area where such equipment can be kept. For example, keep an extra bottle of whiteout, a ruler, a stapler and a pair of scissors on top of a filing cabinet. Make others aware that the equipment in this area is theirs, while your desk is *yours*.

People have the psychological upper hand when they're in their own territory. Salespeople are very aware of this. If the client comes to the seller's place of business, the seller has the advantage. If the salesperson goes to the potential client's place of business, the client has the advantage. That is why salespeople often try to find a neutral ground on which to sell their products.

This psychological truth also holds when a supervisor needs to discipline an employee. If the situation isn't serious, the supervisor will likely go to the employee's territory, so that the employee will feel less threatened, or will arrange to discuss the matter on neutral territory, such as an empty office or cafeteria. Privacy is a must in all cases.

With a more serious problem, the supervisor will most likely have the employee come to his or her office, where s/he will have more power and the employee will feel less secure. There are degrees of intimidation here, too. For the employee, the least threatening environment in the supervisor's office is at a round table of some sort. Next is beside the supervisor's desk. In the most threatening arrangement, the supervisor is behind the desk with the subordinate sitting opposite. To increase the quelling effect the supervisor might arrange for the subordinate to sit in a lower chair than the supervisor. Or a supervisor who is small in stature might stand up to give a more powerful impression.

Eye Contact

Variations in eye contact convey a great deal. Comfortable direct eye-to-eye contact is three seconds. If you hold eye contact longer than three seconds, you are invading another's body space as directly as if you had touched him or her. Many aggressive people use a fixed stare to intimidate others. They could be thirty metres away from you, but you'd still feel their invasion of your space.

You may have used extended eye contact yourself when you've been very angry with someone. You looked them right in the eye as you spoke to them. If the person says, *"He was shooting darts at me,"* that person was probably giving full eye contact for too long, possibly reinforced by an angry expression.

Blinking eyes may indicate either lying or nervousness. Unblinking eyes with eye contact could mean the person is lying and watching for your reaction. Or the person could be intensely interested in what you're saying.

A wink can show either intimacy or lack of seriousness. The latter may be directed at parents when you're telling a *"white lie"* to their child.

Arguments

Should you have to referee an argument, put your knowledge of body language to the test. The body language of bystanders observing the argument can tell you what the observers believe and whose side they're on. If they've had the opportunity of learning the facts of the case, they'll automatically take sides. When this happens, they'll copy the body language of the person they think is in the right. The more observers there are the better, because they'll unknowingly choose sides. You'll then have a running start on refereeing the argument.

CHAPTER FIVE
DEALING WITH CLIENTS

Customer Service

Customer service is more important today than it was in the past. When clients are asked why they purchase a product or service, most of them say that their decision was heavily influenced by the quality of service provided by the client.

If you're like me and run into someone who doesn't answer the phone properly, or handles clients in less than a professional manner, your impression of the entire company goes rapidly downhill.

How can you provide TLC (tender loving care) when something's gone wrong and the customer is upset?

Saying, *"I can see you're upset about this - let's see what I can do to fix things,"* can go a long way towards calming the customer down.

Some employees give the impression that looking after a client is an interruption to their *real* work. Employees may forget is that *"the customer is always number one."* The customer's needs should take precedence over any other work the employee has.

Customer service revolves around - empathy - empathy and more empathy! Customers appreciate courtesy in the service provided to them. Such behaviour implies that the employee is doing clients a favour by helping them.

If you work in the service industry, ask yourself this question, *"Do I like serving people? Do I want to make their day better than it was before they met me?"* If your honest answer is *"No,"* please do everyone a favour and get out of the service industry!

Unfortunately, many people are employed in the service industry simply *"because the job was available."* These people should be employed elsewhere.

One goal society should have, is to create a way of life that allows people to serve others without feeling subservient. Some men may feel that serving others (either at home or on the job) is demeaning or *"women's work."* They believe they'll lose their masculinity if they serve others.

Your tone of voice and body language give you away. There's a tremendous difference between starting a conversation with a curt *"Yes?"* and smiling while saying, *"Good morning, how may I help you today?"* In a department-store study, I found that six out of ten shop assistants never smiled. They gave the impression they were doing customers a favour by waiting on them.

Customer service isn't just important for those who work in stores and restaurants. Every kind of organisation that exists in society needs proper customer service. Rudeness, impatience and insensitivity aren't compatible with good, professional sales. Even so, salespeople display many of these negative traits for a wide range of reasons. Discourtesy, disrespect, indifference, slow service, ignorance of the services offered by the company. Errors and negative behaviour repel customers and leave bad feelings. Customers often respond to bad feelings by simply staying away.

Customers gravitate to places where they get the most positive feelings. The way employees behave with customers is far more important than all the company money spent on advertising and image building.

How can you improve customer service? If you spend time thinking about the ways you can give better service and make customers happier, you'll achieve success wherever you work.

The most successful members of service organisations share common traits. They learn everything they possibly can about their organisation and how it can serve its clients better.

Knowledgeable employees know:
- What their organisation does;
- Who their key personnel are;

- Why the organization works the way it does;

- What service or product the organisation offers;

- What common questions or problems are likely to arise; and

- How they can help clients most effectively.

Successful employees also manage to find out what customers want, expect and need. They go out of their way to do this by asking questions and really listening to the answers. They anticipate questions about the product or service the company offers.

Do you listen to your customers and honestly try to help them? Keep them informed about what you're doing to meet their needs? Let them know exactly what to anticipate? People almost always accept accurate estimates or honest reasons for delays.

You may think of your job as dull and routine, but you insult your clients if you make them feel as if they're not important or if you look bored with your job. Clients stop buying or switch their buying habits if salespeople don't make the buying experience a pleasant one.

Again, trying to put yourself in the customer's place, consider for a moment whether you've encountered the following situations in the past:

- You're five years old, and you've been waiting at the ice cream counter watching much taller people (who came in after you) being served before you.

- You go into a restaurant, sit down and watch others being served. Some people who came in after you are halfway through their meal, before your order is taken.

- You go into a department store and stand quietly while the assistants have their little chitchat before acknowledging you.

- You get gas and have your oil checked. Later you find that the attendant has left oily fingerprints all over your newly washed car.

- You've booked a room but receive sceptical looks from the front-desk clerk, who can't find your hotel reservation.

- It's raining heavily, and you struggle with a rental car released without windshield washer fluid.

- You order from room service at 7:00 a.m. and do without your breakfast because it doesn't arrive before you need to leave for an 8:30 meeting.

- You're short of cash so write a cheque to yourself. You present it to a teller of your own bank where you're a regular customer. The teller gives you suspicious looks and demands two pieces of personal identification,

I'm sure many of these examples strike a chord with you. Companies should be more aware that a poorly served customer may never come back to use their services. It amuses me to see businesses spending huge sums to get customers back who might never have left if they'd received better service and a little courtesy. That is all your clients expect of you as well.

Real damage is caused when customers storm out of the shop. Not only do many not come back, but they tell all their friends about the poor service too. If an angry customer comes to you for help, you have the ideal opportunity to prevent that damage. The real disaster hasn't happened yet. If you handle the situation correctly, it *won't* happen. Remember, once you've lost a customer, it's twice as hard to get him or her back.

Have you ever left a store (even though you wanted to buy something) simply because you were not able to get proper service? If customers know they will receive good service, they may be prepared to pay more for an item or accept a substitute instead of their first choice.

When I'm dissatisfied with service or don't get what I require from a company, I have two choices; (a) I can decide never to go back, or (b) I can give them a second chance.

I've learned to give companies a second chance by complaining to someone who's able to correct the situation. I had received poor service with an airline. Instead of making my travel arrangements with another airline (a definite alternative), I chose to speak to the supervisor of the offending ticket agent. I explained my dilemma to the supervisor who made the following comment, *"If you're happy with our service, tell everyone. If you're dissatisfied with our service, please tell me - because I'm in a position to do something about it."* He promised to speak to his employee about the problem.

Here are a few situations that may have happened to you. See what you would do:

1) You work for a company that supplies auto parts. You're waiting on clients at the front desk, and a man rushes in. He knows that you're dealing with another customer. He gives the impression that he's in a hurry by shifting his weight from foot to foot, looking at his watch, and sighing. How can you make his wait a little easier?

   Remember that there's nothing more frustrating than waiting impatiently for a person to assist you and that person doesn't seem to know you're there. Your first step should be to acknowledge the client's presence. You can do this by saying, *"I'll be with you in a moment."*

2) You finish with your original client. You nod to the man, and he comes up to the counter. What should you say to him, to make him feel better about having to wait?

   Say, *"Thank you for your patience. What can I do for you today?"*

3) The client shows you a form he has completed that he received in the mail. But someone has sent the wrong order form to him. You explain that it's the wrong form, and he becomes very angry. What should you reply?

   Your first impulse might be to say, *"Well, I wasn't responsible for sending you the wrong form"* (defend yourself), or, *"George must have sent it by mistake"* (blaming someone else)? Would that make him happy? Of course not! He doesn't care who sent him the wrong form, he just wants his car parts!

What you should say is, *"I'm sorry you received the wrong form. I don't blame you for being upset; I would be too if that had happened to me. Let me help you fill out the correct form."*

In this transaction, you didn't pass the buck. Not only have you apologised for the error and empathised with the person, but also, you've taken active steps to correct the problem.

4) Suppose it was you who sent the wrong form to them? Do you say, *"We've just changed our system, and don't use that form anymore"* (passing the buck)? Or do you admit your error, *"I'm sorry, I made a mistake. This is the form I should have sent to you. Let me save you some time by helping you fill it out."*

Dealing with angry clients

Remind yourself that angry clients probably have a need that isn't being met and believe you have the ability at least to start the problem on the way to being solved. However, you may find it more effective *not* to focus immediately on solving the problem.

- How do you handle a situation where a client is yelling at you?

- What is your immediate reaction?

- What's happening to you physically, mentally, emotionally? (fight or flight syndrome).

- Do you feel as if you're in control during the situation?

- How could you maintain the control of a volatile situation like that?

First, deal with clients' feelings. Use empathy - put yourself in their shoes. Say such things as, *"I don't blame you for being upset. I'd feel that way too if that had happened to me"*. Listen carefully, maintaining eye contact, nodding your head, etc. Ask questions to clarify matters for yourself; *"And then what happened?"* or *"Did the item not fit properly?"* Then give the client feedback on what you understand the problem (or cause of anger) to be.

Then, deal with their problem. Once you've dealt with the clients' feelings, you're now ready to deal with their problem. Find out what they want from you. Say something like, *"I see we have a problem here. What would you like me to do to help you?"*

Many employees forget to ask this question, but it is a very powerful problem-solving tool. Often clients don't really know what they want from you. You should then clarify what is really being requested and take steps to solve the problem.

What could you say if you can't do what the person wants? If you just tell someone that you can't meet his or her needs, the person will be understandably unhappy. However, if you can offer alternatives, the person will be less unhappy. Whenever you can't meet a client's needs, tell the person what you *can* do that comes closest to meeting the need. Give the person at least two alternatives, but not more than three. (Any more than three is confusing). What you've done is return the control of the situation to the client. In the client's mind, s/he is now back in the driver's seat. The result is a win-win situation.

If there aren't any alternatives, explain the company rules and/or policies that make it impossible to meet the client's request. Explain only what's applicable to the person's own situation. Then work with the client to come up with a course of action (or an alternative you've suggested) so you both understand what's to happen. Make sure you follow up and do what you've said you'll be doing. Give the personal finishing touch by urging customers to contact you should they have problems in the future.

Note: Keep in mind that all problems aren't this easy to solve. You may not be able to satisfy customers fully, but you can try to negotiate with them so there's no winner or loser.

Suppose that a client starts to shout at you, really takes a strip off you for something that wasn't your fault. What would your natural reaction be?

1. You defend yourself or your company

Most of us respond this way. The client attacked you verbally, which triggered your defence mechanism. This response is instinctive, as natural for you as breathing. When you respond defensively, does it usually solve anything? Not likely. Is this going to satisfy the customer? Not likely. You could end up in a shouting match, resulting in negative feelings in each party. This is a lose - lose situation.

2. You're furious at the client's behaviour but grit your teeth and concentrate on solving the problem.

Even though you don't show it on the outside, inside you're seething. If you absorb their anger, it will have to be removed later. Some bark at the next person they see, drive like a maniac on the way home from work or go home and kick the dog or yell at the children. Remember, you choose whether to accept the person's anger or not.

You've allowed the situation to get to you. This is also a negative response - in this case, for you. Stop for a moment and ask yourself, *"What is the client angry at - me or the situation?"* In most cases, you'll find it's the situation. You happen to be there, so you become the recipient of the client's frustration and anger.

3. Before responding, you take time to recognize that the client is angry at the situation, not you. Therefore, there is no need for you to defend yourself.

This last solution works best. You accomplish this by stopping your defence mechanism from kicking in. It's easier to do this than you think. It takes practice - but you can do it if you set your mind to it! As soon as you feel yourself getting uptight and feel the need to defend yourself, stop and analyse the situation. The customer is upset at your company or the situation - not at you. There is absolutely no need for you to defend yourself. Instead, you can concentrate on solving the client's problem. The client ends up happy and so do you - a win - win situation.

You choose the correct approach by concentrating on the client's problem, rather than your own feelings. You accomplish this by:

- Taking notes while the person is talking;
- Using paraphrasing to be sure that you understand the person's problem. This proves that you have been listening to what s/he is saying;
- Asking questions.

Passing the buck, saying you're not responsible, or defending your company is not the answer. The customer doesn't care whether the mistake is yours or someone else's; s/he just wants you to remove the problem. You'll stay calmer if you don't take a defensive stance. Usually, when you've solved the problem, the client will say, *"I'm sorry I shouted at you."*

Here are some of the frustrations (which can lead to anger) clients and customers have identified:

Their Need: Good customer service, but

Blocks:

No one listens to me!

Something went wrong.

I'm not getting your help.

The product doesn't work.

Satisfaction of Need: Someone helps me

Your first step should be to determine what the customer's block is. Then you can concentrate on the problem.

If a client believes that *"No-one listens to me,"* and takes out his or her frustration by shouting at you, how can you show that you're listening? Your body language would show this, and you would paraphrase what you believe they have said. Then you would ask questions to learn more about their problem. This would also assist in dealing with *"Something went wrong," "I'm not getting your help,"* and *"The product doesn't work."*

To remove client blocks:

1. Turn off your defense mechanism.

2. Listen carefully to what they say.

3. Paraphrase what they've said.

4. Ask questions.

5. Do your best to solve their problem.

How to deal with angry clients

1. Acknowledge that they're there.

2. Deal with the person's feelings.

3. Deal with the person's problem.

4. If you can't do what they want you to do, give alternatives (at least two)

5. If your company caused the problem, apologize - don't blame others.

6. Don't be afraid to admit that you made a mistake.

General principles and techniques

For some of us, the most difficult and exasperating people are clients and customers. Companies usually forbid their employees to retaliate when faced with client's negative behaviour. The result is often frustrated, stressed-out employees.

Those who work on the front lines representing their company are susceptible to losing their cool. This is especially true if they need to deal on the phone or in person with angry or dissatisfied clients. Clients who have a complaint may be irritable, rude, impatient, persistent, emotional or aggressive. They often choose a representative of the company (possibly *you*) as the butt of their anger. How you handle their problem makes all the difference to how both of you feel. Let's put ourselves in the customer's place for a minute.

Dealing with language barriers

Until they become completely fluent in English, people who speak English as a second language normally go through the following process:

Stage 1. They hear what you say in English.

Stage 2. They translate what you've said into their first language.

Stage 3. They construct their answer in their first language.

Stage 4. They reply to you in English.

You can see that this process takes time, so if you're conversing with someone whose second language is English, try to:

1. Use simple, ordinary language. You can't expect them to learn jargon or technical language right away.

2. Watch their body language. If they frown, you may have lost them, or they may be going through the above process. If they don't reply within a reasonable length of time, repeat what you said, using simpler language.

3. Allow them time to interpret what you've said. The *"pregnant pause"* between the end of your speech and the beginning of their responses may be necessary for complete understanding on their part.

Sometimes, no matter what you do, you may find it impossible to understand what someone is saying to you. Whenever possible try to find someone who speaks the person's language. If that's not possible, ask the person to bring someone (perhaps a child or a relative) who can act as an interpreter. If this is a recurring problem, check government offices to see if they have interpreters to translate. Refer the caller to this service. Catch yourself if you have guilt feelings. If you've done everything you can to understand the person, you have no reason to accept any guilt feelings.

Dealing with persistent people

In this age of telemarketing, we've all encountered telephone salespeople. For example, you're probably familiar with the sweet young thing that wants to explain her company's rug-cleaning special. When she identifies herself and asks how your day is going, you know that a sales pitch will follow. I suggest using the following technique:

The stuck record technique

This technique also works well in an office if you're the one who needs to fend off salespeople. Let's say your instructions are to accept only a person's business card and catalogue (or information on their product or service). Someone from you company will follow-up if the offered product or service is of interest.

With the stuck-record technique, you simply repeat the same thing. You don't raise your voice or get defensive. By the third refusal, the salesperson usually accepts that you're serious.

Here's an example of how to deal with telemarketers:

"We have a special on rug-cleaning today."

"Thank you for calling, but I'm not interested."

"But this special is just good for this week..."

"I'm not interested."

"How about having your living-room suite cleaned?"

"I'm not interested... Goodbye." You hang up.

Many might feel that this person is just trying to make a living. My answer to this is that they're invading my privacy. If I want rug cleaning, I'll call and ask for it.

Here's how to handle the next salesperson:

"I'd like to see the office manager please."

"Do you have an appointment?"

"No, I don't."

"Could you please tell me the reason for your visit?"

"I'd like to explain our product to your office manager?"

"My instructions are to accept any information you'd care to leave. The office manager will call you if she's interested."

"Our special is only on this week."

"Leave the information with me, and the office manager will call you if she's interested."

"I'm sure she would want to see me."

"Leave the information with me and the office manager will call you if she's interested [you hold out a hand for the information]. Thank you."

You can use this technique in other instances too – for instance, when someone is trying to convince you to do something you really don't want to do:

"Harry, can you drive me home from work tonight?"

"No, I can't, sorry, I'm busy."

"Harry, I really need you to drive me from home from work tonight. How come you can't drive me?"

"As I said, I'm too busy."

When anyone asks you to explain why you've said no, they're acting aggressively and are trying to take advantage of you. You're under no obligation to tell people why you can't do what they want you to do. Use this technique whenever you want to say *"No"* to somebody who's trying to convince you to say *"Yes."* No guilt feelings.

Using the stuck-record technique

"I have to enforce rules and regulations on my clients. They don't like many of these rules, and I feel pressured when they insist that I make exceptions for them."

This is just one of the many problems that are most effectively dealt with by using the stuck-record technique.

For example, you could say, *"I understand your frustration, but I can't make exceptions for anyone."* Or, *"I'd like to make an exception in this case, but I can't."* If the person continues to complain, calmly repeat exactly what you said before. Repeat it again if the person continues to badger you. Don't raise your voice or get defensive. You'll find that the third time you make the comment - the client will hear you. But remember: when you can't do what a person wants, try to give them at least two alternative solutions if possible.

Correcting your own mistakes

Do you have the problem admitting you made a mistake? We all make them, and most of us hate to admit it. But when someone makes a mistake and acknowledges it, doesn't your respect for that person go up? Most people wrongly assume that others will respect them less if they admit to a mistake. The opposite is true.

What can you do when *you* made the mistake? First, don't be ashamed to admit it. Then state, *"I'm sorry that happened. Let's see what I can do to correct the error."* Then correct your mistake. Don't feel you have to defend yourself with such statements as, *"We've been frantically busy. That's why I made a mistake."* Whatever you do, don't ignore the problem; that will just compound the client's anger at both you and your company.

You've blundered, admitted it and you're willing to fix the problem. That works far better for both of you. If the client continues to argue, say, *"What would you like me to do to solve this problem?"*

Using the telephone

If you're like me and run into someone who doesn't answer the phone properly, your impression of the whole company goes rapidly downhill. Remember, if you answer the phone incorrectly, you're likely to turn off potential and even regular customers.

Creating a favourable impression for your firm is imperative. You may be the first and, in some cases, the only contact the customer or client has with your firm. Here are some suggestions:

Telephone Etiquette

1. Answer calls promptly - on the first ring if possible.
2. Transfer calls effectively (see *"telephone responses"*).

3. Give progress reports to callers if they're on hold.

4. Never put your hand over the mouthpiece. (The client will think you're being sneaky or that you're talking about them).

5. No matter how you're feeling at that moment, don't pass your bad mood on to your customer.

6. Keep your cool with difficult customers.

7. *Apologise if you've made a mistake.*

8. Try to give that little extra service to customers that they'll remember in the future.

9. Learn the correct way of making and logging long distance phone calls.

10. Learn the techniques of feedback and paraphrasing so messages aren't misunderstood.

11. When taking a person's name, ask them to spell it for you. Then in brackets, add the phonetic sound of their name so you won't mispronounce it later.

12. If you leave your workstation, make sure you let the receptionist know, or have someone else answers your phone or turn on your voice mail.

13. Keep paper and pen next to *every* telephone.

14. If you must leave the phone to get information, ask whether the caller would rather wait, or should you call him or her back.

15. If callers ask you for information you can't provide, tell them you'll get back to them with the answer. Either return the call yourself or have someone do it that's more familiar with the subject than you. But make sure someone follows-up. The latter suggestion may be preferable when the person may have additional questions during the conversation, which you wouldn't be able to answer.

16. Use the caller's name whenever practical (don't overdo this though). Practice the correct pronunciation of their name.

17. Make long distance calls yourself. Having your secretary do this often wastes the client's time. This suggests to others that you think their time is less valuable than yours.

18. Have notes ready, related to the call being made, so you won't forget important details. If the call needs to be returned, these notes will help you remember everything you wished to discuss.

19. Identify yourself when you answer the phone, e.g., *"Bill Baker, Shipping Department."* Remember, you want to be both polite and pleasant, and want the caller to feel important. You want to avoid wasting the caller's time and the company's time. And, above all, you want to help the caller achieve the purpose of the call.

With a few standard responses, you can meet all these goals in most of the situations you will encounter. A number of these standard responses are outlined below.

Telephone Responses

Situation: Answering an incoming call.
Response: Accounting Department, Bill Jones speaking.

Situation: The person called is on another line.
Response: Bill Jones is talking on another line. Would you like to hold, or may I ask him to call you?

Situation: The person called is away from his or her desk for a few minutes.
Response: Bill Jones is not in his office right now. May I take a message?

Situation: The caller reached the wrong extension.
Response: Our accounting department handles that information. May I transfer you?

Situation: The person called is in a meeting until 3:00 p.m.
Response: Bill Jones is attending a meeting until 3:00 p.m. May I ask him to call you?

Situation: The person called is with a client.
Response: Bill Jones is with a client. May I ask him to call you?

Situation: The person called has left the office for the afternoon.
Response: Bill Jones won't be back this afternoon. Would you like him to call you tomorrow?

Situation: You need to know who is calling.
Response: May I please tell Bill Jones who's calling please?

Situation: The person called is not in yet.
Response: Bill Jones is not in the office just now. May I ask him to call you? (Avoid saying *"He hasn't come in yet today,"* which makes it appear as if he has slept in.)

Situation: The person called is ill.
Response: Bill Jones isn't in today. May I ask him to call you, or could someone else help you?

Situation: You need to give the caller a progress report.
Response: Bill Jones is still on his line. May I take a message, or ask him to call you?

Situation: You are returning to a call on hold.
Response: Thank you for waiting.

Situation: The person called is out of town.
Response: Bill Jones is out of the office until June 4th. May I take a message, or could someone else help you? (Avoid saying, *"He's out of town,"* which could tell burglars it's safe to break into his home.)

Situation: You are answering a call transferred to you.
Response: Accounting Department, Bill Jones speaking. May I help you?

Situation: The person called is out of the office but will be returning.
Response: Carolyn Jones is away from the office until 2:00 p.m. May I have her call you when she returns? (Avoid saying *"I have no idea where she is."* This sounds very unprofessional. You *should* know where she is!)

Situation: The person called is out for coffee.
Response: I expect Bill Jones in about twenty minutes. May I ask him to call you?

Situation: The person called is out for lunch.

Response: I expect Bill Jones at about 1:00 p.m. May I ask him to call you? (Don't say he's *"Out to lunch,"* which could mean to some people that he's missing brainpower.)

Situation: The person called is busy and doesn't want to be disturbed.

Response: Bill Jones isn't available until 3:00 p.m. Could someone else help you, or may I take a message and have him return your call? (Saying *"He's tied up right now,"* brings up images of someone being tied up with ropes.)

Situation: You are completing a phone call.

Response: Thank you for calling. Goodbye.

Situation: You are placing a call.

Response: Good morning. This is Bill Jones of the XYZ Company calling. May I speak with Gordon Smith, please?

Never give replies like, *"She left for lunch about half an hour ago. Call back in two hours, she'll probably be back by then."* Or, *"Today's Thursday and she seldom gets in before 10:30 on Thursday."* Such replies create a poor impression of the person called and, ultimately, of the company as well.

One answer that covers a multitude of situations is, *"I'm sorry Bill Jones isn't available right now."* Bill Jones might be sitting right beside you, but he's *"not available"* to the caller. This makes it unnecessary for receptionists and secretaries to lie for their supervisors. Use this when your supervisor wants you to say, untruthfully, that s/he is not in the office.

Using common sense and good manners

Here are situations where good old common sense should prevail:

1. Your supervisor has tackled a mountain of work and has left word you're not to disturb him unless the building is on fire. The president of your company phones and asks to speak to your supervisor. There are exceptions to every rule. This is obviously one of them.

2. You always seem to receive wrong-number phone calls for another firm with a similar phone number. Don't waste

time feeling angry. Instead, look up the number of the company and be ready to give the right number to the caller.

3. Your municipal government department is like another department in the federal government. People seem to think you're able to answer their questions. Have a set spiel explaining the differences in your functions and give callers the correct number. Don't lose your cool - they're not trying to annoy you.

4. You need to escort a visitor from the reception area to your supervisor's office. Do you:
   a. Precede the visitor, stating, *"Will you follow me, please"?*
   b. Let the visitor go first, stating, *"It's down this corridor, first door on your right"?*
   The correct answer is (a)

5. You bring a visitor to your supervisor's office. They've never met before. Do you:
   a. Let the visitor walk in?
   b. Announce the visitor, saying *"[Supervisor's name], this is Bill Jones from XYZ Company"*
   c. Introduce each to the other?
   The correct answer is (b).

6. Your supervisor calls you into her office while she has a male visitor. The visitor stands when you enter. Should you:
   a. Nod at the visitor, and sit down?
   b. Nod at the visitor, and say, *"Won't you please be seated?"*
   c. Say, *"Hello,"* and sit down?
   Both (a) and (c) are correct.

7. Your supervisor's spouse drops in just before closing time. Should you:
   a. Call your supervisor on the intercom and follow the instructions given?
   b. Offer the visitor a chair in the reception area?

c. Smile and make small talk until your supervisor is available?

The correct answer is (a) unless your supervisor is unavailable for a while, then (b) is correct.

CHAPTER SIX

OTHER TYPES OF CLIENT PROBLEMS

The client has already had the run-around

You answer the phone for your company. The person on the phone is really upset. She has had the proverbial run-around. She says, *"You're the fourth person I've spoken to without getting any answers. Can't anyone help me?"*

This person has been the victim of the pas-the-buck syndrome, and the buck should stop with you. Saying, *"Sorry, this is the wrong department again,"* isn't going to be acceptable. She wants her problem solved, and she sees you as being able to help her. She doesn't care if it's *"your department"* or not. She was frustrated when she first called, but she's now well on her way to becoming unglued. If you also lose your cool and become angry, the problem will get even worse.

Out-of-control anger can be compared to temporary insanity. If possible, try to prevent your client from becoming temporarily insane, or bring her back to sanity if she's already there. You do this by starting the problem on its way to being solved. If you can do *anything* to move towards a solution, the client will appreciate your help.

Obtaining all the pertinent information necessary to get the person helped could do this. Then ask for the person's telephone number and have the appropriate employee call her back *within a reasonable length of time!* If the employee can't respond right away, keep the client informed. Give the client your name and number so she can call you back if she doesn't obtain satisfaction from your reference person. Then and only then are you off the hook with the client.

The client acts like the "class clown"

Class clowns are difficult to handle. In school, they're the ones who disrupt the class and keep things in an uproar. The aim of this behaviour is to get attention. Children who are class clowns crave any attention they can get and are perfectly willing to accept negative attention rather than have none.

How do experienced teachers handle this kind of child? They give the child the attention it craves - but for *good* behaviour. When the child misbehaves, it is isolated from the rest of the class (the opposite of what it wants). Usually the teacher will take the child away from the group and quietly speak to the offender.

When these children become adults, their class-clown behaviour often continues. They're the people who make sure everyone in the room knows how annoyed they are at something your company has done. They're the ones who want immediate attention. If they don't get it, they become verbally abusive and upset everyone around them.

How do you handle these people? The same way you treat children who exhibit this kind of negative behaviour. Take them aside, preferably into a private office. (Don't attempt this if they look physically abusive.) Explain to them that you'll be happy to handle their problem as soon as it's their turn, that if they continue their unacceptable behaviour, you'll be forced to ignore them. Then return them to the area where they were waiting and handle the next customer.

Obviously, before you attempt the above, you should have your supervisor's full approval. If you don't you may find yourself in the middle if the client decides to go higher with the problem. If you regularly have behavioural problems to deal with, discuss tactics with your supervisor. Review possible strategies and obtain your supervisor's suggestions on how to handle problems. Both of you will then know that difficult situations will be handled consistently.

The client refuses to deal with a woman

Sally Brown, who's the credit manager for a large construction firm, solved the problem she was facing in a rather humorous way. She had to put up with what seemed like too many clients who insisted on *"talking to a man."* She solved the problem by patching the calls through to Sam, the janitor in the building.

Sam had been clued in and knew how to handle that kind of call. His standard reply was, *"I don't know why you're talking to me. Sally Brown's our credit manager. I'll transfer you back and she can look after you."*

Another solution would be for Sally to answer her phone by identifying herself clearly. She should say, *"Sally Brown, Credit Manager, how may I help you?"* Most people assume that you're in a low-level position if you answer your phone by just your first name. Most men answer with their full name and title. Women should do the same to receive the respect they deserve.

The client blames you for someone else's mistake

"I had a problem last week that reduced me to tears. I'm the stockroom clerk in a warehouse of our company. I haven't been on the job for long, and the warehouse manager left me in charge while he picked up some equipment. An angry client phoned in to complain that we had delivered the wrong part and it was costing his company a mint. He called me stupid and acted as if it was my entire fault!

He had ordered the part two months before I even started with the company! I kept insisting that he would have to phone back in fifteen minutes when the warehouse manager returned. I used the stuck-record technique, but it didn't seem to work. How could I have handled this irate customer?"

In this case, I can see why the stuck-record technique didn't work. You forgot to turn off your defence mechanism when the client started yelling at you. What you could have done was take down information as soon as the person started talking. You would have paraphrased and asked questions that would have assisted in solving his problem.

As it was, when the warehouse manager returned fifteen minutes later, no one had started to solve the person's problem. It's likely the manager had to deal with an even angrier client fifteen minutes later! If you had obtained the pertinent information, the warehouse manager would have had some answers for the irate client when he returned his call.

Remember this whenever taking a complaint call for another person.

You should also be careful in giving a timeline about when the warehouse manager will be returning. If you say he'll be back in fifteen minutes, and he doesn't get back for half an hour - you can bet the client will call back within that second fifteen minutes.

The client drops in without an appointment

"How should I handle regular clients who just drop in, expecting someone to see them?"

Using the stuck-record technique, tell them, *"I'm sorry; you can't see Bill Jones without an appointment. Would you like to make one for another time?"* If the client objects, say, *"My instructions are that no one's seen unless s/he has an appointment. Would you like to make an appointment for another time?"*

The client is long-winded

"I handle a busy switchboard. When callers want to give me their life story, how can I handle them tactfully?"

Sometimes, it's necessary to interrupt them (they do have to come up for air). Ask if they can *briefly* explain the problem because you'll be passing them on to another person.

"I have a client whom I can't keep on track. He's always going off topic."

When dealing with a compulsive talker, use every conversational gap to guide the conversation towards accomplishing the needs of the phone call. Never show your boredom or frustration, as it'll offend the client. If you give alternatives, the client can make some decisions. Summarise your conversation, stating what you'll be doing for them, or what they'll be doing for you. Then use this closing clincher: *"I believe we've covered everything. I won't take up any more of your valuable time."*

The client needs an immediate answer

"I work in a by-law office, and people phoning in need information immediately. I can't contact the by-law officer because he's out of the office."

One solution is to have a beeper for the by-law officer. Another is to have the officer phone in on a regular basis to obtain messages. The ideal answer is for him to carry a mobile phone when he leaves the office. Use feedback with the by-law officer to explain the problems you're having with clients and ask for his or her assistance in finding solutions.

The client is a know-it-all

"I have trouble dealing with know-it-all people who ask you for information, but really just want to give their own version of what's right."

First, listen to the client's ideas and ask for any facts that support those views. Then, using the information available to you, tell the client the real facts. Refer to rules, regulations, policies and procedure manuals or other written data if necessary.

The client is condescending or rude

"How do I deal with people who are condescending to me - treat me like dirt? They give me the impression that because I'm a clerk I don't know anything. They usually come in to get information regarding college courses."

These are people who probably lack self-assurance and try to put you down to make themselves feel more important. They may or may not use sarcasm to do this. Turn off your defence mechanism. Realize that you are in control of the situation. After all, *they* are coming to *you* for information. Just give them the information they request. Don't allow them to make you lose their cool. You might ask them the show-stopping question, *"What do you want me to do to solve this problem?"* This often stops them long enough to clarify what they really want from you.

"I have a client who's very rude to me every time he calls in but is as sweet as pie to my boss. How can I get this person to treat me better?"

Using feedback and the expression, *"I have a problem and I need your help in solving it..."* explain to your supervisor the rudeness of the client. Ask your supervisor to speak to this person about the matter. The client should know that this is unacceptable behaviour to any employee of the company. If your supervisor won't back you up, transfer this person's call directly to the supervisor without having any further exchange with that person.

The client puts your long-distance call on hold

"When I call long distance, I get furious if the receptionist puts me on hold without asking whether I object. How can I deal with being put on "ignore" in the future?"

If this is a regular occurrence, talk to the receptionist's supervisor and explain the inconvenience and costs this delay gives you. I jump right in and say that my call is long-distance even before identifying whom I am calling. I say, *"Long distance for Marie Baker."* They assume I'm a long-distance operator and put the call through right away. A more drastic solution is to bill this client for the time you were put on hold.

The client refuses to wait his or her turn

"My boss, a lawyer, is very busy. Last week. A friend of his needed some legal advice and expected service immediately. I explained the situation and suggested that he make an appointment. The friend barged right into my boss's office, where he was in a meeting with a client. How could I have handled that situation better?"

Talk to your supervisor and ask what you should do if a similar situation happens in the future. Unless you had used some fast judo or karate, the friend would have been in your supervisor's office before you could react anyway. Throw your guilt trip out the window. At the time, you did the best you could to handle the situation.

The client uses profane language or threatening behaviour

"What should I do when my caller uses profane language on the phone? Do I have to put up with that kind of garbage?"

I don't believe anyone should have to put up with profane language. You should be able to hang up on the caller. Check with your supervisor to see what you're expected to do. It's possible, because of the work you do, that you do have to put up with that kind of garbage - for instance, if you're working in an emergency ward of a hospital. It's part of the pattern for some people to start swearing when upset about something. You can't just refuse to handle the problem of this upset person. If you're working on a crisis or emergency line of any kind, you must know that this language may go with the territory. You may, however, ask such callers to clean up their language so you can handle their difficulty better. But above all, make sure you know what your supervisor wants you to do.

You must deal with two clients simultaneously

"I never know whether I should handle the person on the phone or the person who has waited to see me for fifteen minutes. Who should get priority?"

Answer the phone and tell the caller you're with a client and will be a few minutes. Give alternatives. Ask whether the caller would like to call back, have you return the call later or be put on hold. Then alternate between those who have come in person and those who phone in.

"I work for a parts department of an auto-supply firm. I'm trying to get them to set up a numbering system, so customers are dealt with in turn. Right now, because it's hard to keep track of who is next (I need to go into the warehouse to get their parts,) I often can't be sure in what order to help people. I've had to referee several battles about whose turn it is and find that it gets me rattled."

After you decided whom you would serve first and had eventually dealt with the two irate customers, you should have reminded yourself, *"That was certainly an unpleasant encounter, but I did the best I could."* Remember, in situations like this, no matter whom you serve first, you're *"damned if you do and damned if you don't."* You have no reason to take on guilt feelings because you couldn't please them both simultaneously. Use feedback with your supervisor to explain the difficulties not having a numbering system is causing you and the rest of the staff. (You could also try setting up an informal numbering system on your own, while you wait for the firm to act.)

How about drunk or threatening people?

This is another topic you must talk about to your supervisor *before* it happens. Know when to call in a security guard or the police. Knowing what steps to take and having an emergency plan of your own makes you more confident when having to deal with such unexpected and unsettling problems.

CHAPTER SEVEN
DEALING WITH SUPERIORS

If you're not enjoying your work, there could be several reasons why. One possible cause of job dissatisfaction is poor supervision. Some individuals have been chosen for their supervisory positions because they know a lot about the type of work done by those they are supervising. They may know next to nothing, however, about how to motivate *people.*

If you think your supervisor's style of managing is responsible for your job dissatisfaction, this chapter is for you.

When I first started offering my *"Dealing with Difficult People"* seminars, I assumed that *"off the wall"* clients would be the most difficult group in the workplace. My second guess was difficult workmates. I was wrong in making those assumptions! I found that overwhelmingly, their supervisors and managers were the most difficult people faced by the 55,000 participants of my seminar! Why is this the case?

Supervisors from Hell

Because most of their supervisors/ managers/ department heads and even executives had not received the basic training necessary for them to successfully supervise others, they described their supervisors as *"Supervisor from Hell"*. These difficult supervisors made the following mistakes,

- Embarrass their staff by disciplining them in front of workmates or clients.
- Label staff's behaviour (stupid, dumb) or make sarcastic remarks, instead of trying to correct the actual behaviour of the staff member.
- Don't give recognition for a job well done. Instead, they concentrate on the two percent of the things their staff do incorrectly, instead of the ninety-eight percent they do properly.
- When dealing with customer complaints, they don't back up their staff and don't give employees a chance to tell

their side of the story before acting. (They should say to the client, *"Let me investigate this and I'll get back to you."*)

- Don't provide an up-to-date job description with key performance indicators and standards of performance for the tasks performed by their staff.
- Don't provide the necessary training to fill the gap between job requirements and employee's skills.
- They have the audacity to conduct performance appraisals on staff without a proper job description upon which to base their evaluation. (If the employee doesn't know what's expected of him/her, and the supervisor doesn't know either - how can a fair evaluation of the performance be conducted?)
- Have one set of company rules for staff - another for themselves. Bend the rules when clients go over the head of front-line staff, causing embarrassment for staff members.
- No set policy and procedure manuals available. Rules and regulations of the company are not clearly defined.
- Harass staff (either through bullying or sexual harassment).
- Do nothing to improve the employee's interest in their jobs. Some are afraid their employees are now ready to compete for their job, so do as little as possible to develop their skills for their next step up. (It's a proven fact that more supervisors are *not* promoted because there is nobody prepared to take over their existing job.)
- Are not available when their staff needs their help. They say they have an *"open door policy,"* but are always *"too busy"* to deal with their staff's problems.
- Won't listen to their staff's suggestions about better ways to complete tasks. The person doing the job normally has the best ideas on how to do the job better, faster, and more efficiently
- Are perfectionists and expect everything to be done perfectly. Just because they can do the job in ten minutes (they have fifteen years' experience) they expect the newcomer to do it in the same amount of time with the same amount of accuracy.

Let's assume you're the new supervisor. You've decided that because you have a B.A. or an MBA degree, you're fully prepared to be a supervisor and you'll be safe if you clone the behaviour of your past supervisors. Unfortunately, most B.A. and MBA degree programs do not include supervisory training, and most supervisors have not had the proper training. Therefore, you may be setting yourself up to be another *"Supervisor from Hell"*.

So, you decide to do the right thing and obtain basic supervisory training. Will it take a long time and cost too much? No - learning the basics of supervision won't involve as much time as you'd expect. What will you need to learn? The first thing you'll realise is that you'll have an entirely different role to play. People will expect so much from you - from your boss downward, and from your staff upwards. How's a person to cope?

You'll be expected to delegate work to your staff, but how do you decide who's the right person to do the job? And after you've delegated the task, how do you motivate your staff to do a good job for you? How do you manage your time, when so many people need you to be available to them - and still get your own work done? You know that if you're not efficient in time management, you'll have your staff sitting around twiddling their thumbs one minute or madly scrambling at the last minute to complete assignments. If this happens, you'll be in trouble with *your* boss.

Then there are the problems - oh the problems! Why do your staff keep coming to you with their *"Mickey Mouse"* problems - can't they use some initiative and make some decisions on their own? You say that if I'd trained them thoroughly - they wouldn't be coming to me with those kinds of problems? Who has the time or the capabilities to play the part of a training manager along with all the other duties I'm expected to perform?

Am I responsible for choosing new staff? How am I supposed to hire staff when I've never hired anyone before, and haven't a clue how to do so, without breaking the anti-discrimination laws? And you say I'll have to step in and deal with personality problems between staff members, correct behaviour and production problems, update job descriptions, and conduct performance appraisal interviews? How am I going to cope with all these new responsibilities?

Then you need to consider the following. What if you're one of ten workmates who applied for the job, and are facing nine hostile staff members who thought they should have your job? And Margaret is your best friend - can you still socialise with her or will you have to distance yourself from her because she now reports to you?

Many who have taken on the responsibilities of a supervisor wonder what possibly possessed them to accept the position! Unless a supervisor knows how to deal with these issues - s/he will likely become another *"Supervisor from Hell"*. So, what's a person to do? The answer is simple - get the necessary training - even if you need to pay for it yourself!

Poor motivators

Many employees are self-motivating and will work well even under poor supervision. Every employee, however, can respond to and benefit from a supervisor who understands what motivates people to do their best work. Because not every employee is the same, a good supervisor will develop insight into which employees respond best to praise, which to monetary incentives and which to opportunities to learn new things or to prepare for a promotion.

If your motivation at work is suffering, it may be because your supervisor doesn't understand that some or all the following working conditions can have a powerfully *de*-motivating effect.

1. ***Restrictive supervision.*** You'll likely obtain less job satisfaction if your supervisor gives you little chance to take an active part in how you complete your assignments. The more employees participate in how they do things, the more cooperative they will be. Supervisors who use an

authoritarian leadership style are setting themselves up to fail. If you have this type of supervisor, try feedback to alleviate the problem. If your supervisor won't be reasonable and you can't change his or her behaviour, you may have to suffer for a while until a promotion is available. Alternatively, you could take a lateral move to another department or, as a last resort, leave the company you're with.

2. ***Lack of recognition.*** Supervisors de-motivate staff if they identify only what their subordinates have done wrong. They should concentrate instead on what they have done right, to encourage better performance. In the old school of management, supervisors believed it was their right to take credit for new ideas suggested by their subordinates. As you might expect, this just de-motivates employees, discourages new ideas and perpetuates mediocre performance and marginal productivity. Progressive supervisors are learning that if they give employees credit where credit is due, their staff is motivated to perform better. Employees whose supervisors are still stingy with recognition should try using feedback to alleviate this problem. Possibly, the supervisor isn't aware of how de-motivating his or her actions are. Say, *"I have a problem, and I need your help in solving it. In the past week I've gone out of my way to do an exceptional job on the Miller project and have worked overtime to meet the deadline. I'm discouraged because all I've heard about the project is the 2 per cent, I did wrong. What about the 98 per cent I did right? It's not very encouraging to hear only the negatives. Do you understand what I mean?"* This should help the supervisor do a better job in future by giving positive reinforcement when it's due.

3. ***Monotonous work.*** Companies implement job rotation for their employees to make employee's jobs more interesting. Job rotation is possible if there are several employees in a company who work at substantially the same class or level or work and in the same pay range. Employers and employees alike benefit from job rotation, because staff

members can fill more than one job and someone else can do the work of absent employees. If your company is doing this, management is trying to keep your work interesting. If they haven't tried job rotation, suggest they do so, for all your sakes.

4. *Little opportunity to try new ideas.* Employee's motivation also suffers when supervisors ignore workers' suggestions for better ways of doing the jobs. Because the employees are doing the actual work, they are often in the best position to come up with better and quicker ways to do the job. If your supervisor is weak in this area, plant seeds for change slowly. Let him or her get used to the new idea gradually. Use facts to back up your suggestions and identify any cost reduction that can be achieved by doing it the new way. Be open, however, to legitimate reasons why your idea won't work. If your supervisor won't respond to any suggestions, use feedback to describe your frustration.

5. *No opportunities to acquire new skills.* At one time, companies spent many training dollars on their employees and still couldn't keep up with the demand for competent qualified people. Recently, companies have had to tighten their training budgets. Companies may refuse to give training that they believe employees can't use right away. Employees whose promotions are six months to one year away may find it difficult to obtain training. To be sure they are ready for the next step up, employees who find themselves in this position would be wise to obtain and pay for this training themselves. The employee thus gains an edge over others who have not acquired the necessary skills. Dollars spent on training are a good investment by the employee.

6. *Absence of adequate job descriptions and performance appraisals.*

   Companies that practise good management systems know that both accurate, up-to-date job descriptions and performance appraisals are essential for high productivity and motivation of staff. When employees know what's expected of them, they perform better. If more than 10 per cent of your duties fit into the category *"other duties as assigned,"* your job description isn't accurate. How do you go about getting a more realistic one?

Reclassification of position level: If your company is using an official classification system, they know that no more than 10 per cent is allowed under that category. In that case, you could simply itemize your duties and the percentage of your time spent on each item. Your request for reclassification will be based on information. Or, if your job description is more than two years old, it's probably outdated. Again, you need to itemize your duties and the percentage of your time each takes, before pointing out discrepancies between your job description and your actual job and asking for reclassification. A good time to ask for a job-description update is when you have your yearly performance appraisal.

What if tasks are regularly added to your duties without any reclassification of your position? If you are always being given more of the *same* kind of task (job dumping), you can't request a reclassification. But if your new tasks have a different level or responsibility, then your job probably should be reclassified. You would need to use facts to prove that your responsibility level had changed.

In large companies, there are usually formal classification systems. If you work for a small company, you might have some difficulty. Job classification is based on the responsibility level of the tasks performed by the person in the position. If the level of responsibility changes, either upward or downward, the position is usually reclassified. For example, a secretary whose supervisor takes on extra responsibilities will most likely need a job reclassification, because the responsibility level of the secretary rises with the supervisor's. On the other hand, if the supervisor's position is abolished, and the secretary now works for four lower-level people, the responsibility level of the job will be lower, and the position would be reclassified to a lower level.

What if your employer says, *"We don't have job descriptions here?"* In that case, you should write one yourself (using examples found at the library, or accurate descriptions of a friend's position as a guideline). Take it to your supervisor and ask for approval. If approval is refused, ask, *"How can I do a good job for you, if neither of us knows what I'm supposed to do?"*

7. ***Discrepancy between pay and level of responsibility.*** If you're convinced that your salary level is too low for the kind of work you're doing, you'll have to look at your current job description, make any changes necessary, then ask for an appointment with your supervisor. At the meeting, explain that your duties are listed incorrectly and that you have much more responsibility than the description shows. Or perhaps your job description is accurate, but the salary range for it doesn't reflect the job's importance to the company. Find out what similar positions are earning in competitive companies. Expressions such as, *"I think I'm underpaid"* will not help you. Go in equipped with *facts.* You must be able to give reasons to back up your request for more money. If this fails, you may have to leave the company you're with and look elsewhere.

8. ***Unpaid overtime.*** The laws relating to overtime are slightly different. It could be that you should be getting overtime pay if you are putting in extra hours, and I suggest that you contact your regional office of the Department of Wages and Conditions or your Industrial Relations Board of the government to find out exactly what you're entitled to. If you don't know the labour laws in your area, it's up to you to find out.

The aggressive supervisor

In an ideal world, all supervisors would be assertive (rather than passive or aggressive), pleasant, supportive, efficient, tactful and blessed with superior insight into human nature. In the real world, however, supervisors display the usual range of human faults and failings. Supervisors who use aggressive behaviour to dominate and control their staff are among the most difficult for an employee to deal with.

Aggressive supervisors haven't learned one of the fundamentals of good supervision. Employees can't be forced to doing a good job; they're led into it. Supervisors are bound to receive poor productivity from their staff if they:

- Discipline employees publicly;
- Bully them into working excessively long hours;
- Are hypercritical and impossible to please;
- Criticize individuals rather than behaviour.

Before you decide to say anything to an aggressive supervisor, ask yourself if you might make matters worse by saying something. If this person treats *everyone* the same belligerent way, it may not be worth the risk of discussing the matter. You may have to mark time until you can get away from this bully.

If you decide it might help to discuss the problem, use feedback to let your supervisor know how his or her behaviour is affecting you. This takes courage, but at least you will know you tried to improve matters. Talk to your supervisor privately about his or her aggressive behaviour. If the problem is labelling, for example, say, *"I have a problem and I need your help in solving it. I find it difficult to handle the put-downs you've been giving me lately. I can't defend my actions when you call me names. The way it is now, I don't know how to improve my performance or what you really want of me. Could you give me examples of why you think I'm ignorant?"*

If the situation doesn't change, don't go higher up to his or her supervisor to complain. Instead:

- Put up with it if you can, then ask for a transfer to another position in the company;
- Talk to someone in your human resources department; or
- Leave for greener pastures elsewhere.

Go higher up the chain of command only when the supervisor's behaviour is affecting the rest of the staff. Only group complaints can oust a bad supervisor and then only if the complaint is handled correctly. Make sure the group uses facts to explain its grievances. Have details of what has happened, costs in dollars, damage to customer relations, delays, unmet deadlines, unnecessary overtime, production stoppages, etc.

When you feel your supervisor has removed all the pride and pleasure you obtain from your work, then it's time to leave.

As we have seen, aggressive behaviour can take a variety of forms. Ways of dealing with some of these are worth discussing in detail.

Sarcasm

Some sarcasm is nothing more than harmless kidding. It is non-threatening and can be fun. However, sarcasm can also be hurtful, designed to make others feel small. People using it feel a sense of power at seeing other people squirm. Hurtful sarcasm is a form of indirect aggression – one of the sneakiest, most manipulative and underhanded methods of getting your way.

People who use hurtful sarcasm often don't feel very good about themselves, so they attempt to put others down to make themselves feel more important. The game continues when others respond defensively, or act hurt. Sarcastic people want others to get angry and defend themselves. Remind yourself not to respond negatively to their remarks. Try to stick to the facts.

Think for a minute; who's in control in the situation when sarcasm is used? You are (the recipient of the sarcasm) until you reply. Should you respond to sarcasm with more sarcasm? No - if you do, you often just encourage more of the same. Instead, try to analyse why the person might feel the need to put you down. Once you have an idea of what really prompts the sarcasm, you'll be able to deal with the actual issue.

Don't react to sarcasm - turn it off. The sarcastic person won't know what to do, because you're not playing by *"the rules."*

When it's no longer fun to throw things at you, the culprit will take his or her sarcastic remarks elsewhere.

Make aggressive people account for their actions. Often, they aren't aware of how destructive their behaviour is to others.

When I was doing the research for my book, *Escaping the Pink-Collar Ghetto* (now entitled *The Business Women's Bible)* I interviewed more than 700 managers (695 of them men) to see why they weren't promoting more women. Initially, I was met with a crossed-arms defensive stance from most of the managers. I knew they were on the defensive when the sarcasm started to flow. My instinctive reaction was to fight sarcasm with sarcasm, but instead, I stood back from the situation and tried to analyse it. I concluded that these managers felt that when I asked, *"Why aren't you promoting more women?"* that I was accusing them of discriminatory behaviour.

I reassured them by explaining fully what I was there to accomplish; that I really needed their input to find out what "mistakes" women were making that kept them from being promoted. I gave several examples other companies had given me and asked them if the same was true in their company as well. Soon they realised that I was there only to obtain information and their help, not to push them into defending the scarcity of women in senior positions in their company. Most were then very cooperative. They would not have been, however, if I had responded defensively to their sarcasm.

Tantrums

"How do I deal with my boss? He has tantrums on a regular basis. He slams down the phone, bangs his desk drawers, throws things and slams his office door. I'm completely unnerved by his behaviour and become very shaky and nervous. What should I do when this happens in the future?"

Adults who still resort to temper tantrums haven't completely grown up. When it's the supervisor having the tantrum, it's a form of bullying and most employees are protected from that kind of behaviour by law. This woman decided to try to handle the situation herself. A friend advised her to picture her boss wearing a bonnet and diaper, sitting in a high chair, banging a spoon on the tray.

She used this stress reliever the next time he had a tantrum and found that bringing forth this humorous mental image kept her from losing her cool with him. She even had the courage one day (after he had settled down) to ask, *"Are you finished?"*

"Finished what?" He thundered.

"I wondered if you were finished having your temper tantrum?"

He sat quietly for a minute, smiled sheepishly and said, *"I guess that's what you would call it, wouldn't you? Yes, I've finished having my temper tantrum."*

She did the same thing the next time he had a tantrum, with the same smiling reaction, until finally she didn't have to say anything. He would come to his office door and say, *"It's okay now – I'm finished"*. The beautiful spin-off of this situation was that he soon stopped having tantrums entirely.

Humour can get you through many difficult situations. The above example shows that humour can diffuse anger. Somehow, when we're able to laugh about something, the tension lessens. Use funny mental pictures or even place a favourite cartoon near your desk to remind you to see the funny side of situations.

Sexual harassment.

Sexual harassment is usually thought of as a problem for women in the workplace, but men also have unwanted sexual advances directed at them.

This work problem has been affecting employees for centuries. Laws pertaining to harassment are changing rapidly. Whether you're a man or a woman, I urge you to investigate your local legislation. Learn about sexual harassment and how you can reduce it or deal with it. Research shows that 70 to 80 per cent of women have experienced one or more forms of sexual harassment by superiors or co-workers. Fifty-two per cent of them lost or left a job because of it. This should never be tolerated. The use of exit interviews should clear up the issue of why the woman has left her job.

The following types of behaviour can all be regarded as sexual harassment;

- Unwelcome sexual remarks such as jokes, innuendo, teasing and verbal abuse;

- Taunts about a person's body, attire, age, marital status;

- Displays of pornographic or offensive pictures;

- Practical jokes that cause awkwardness or embarrassment;

- Unwelcome invitations or requests, whether indirect or explicit;

- Intimidation;

- Leering or other suggestive gestures.

- Condescending or paternalistic treatment that undermines self-respect;

- Unnecessary physical contact, such as touching, patting, pinching, punching or physical assault.

A related problem is a type of reverse discrimination that occurs when promotions and bonuses are awarded to an employee in return for sexual favours, while other employees who have earned recognition through good work are passed over.

If you are the object of sexual harassment you should:

1. Tell the person that you object to whatever s/he is doing or saying. Let him or her know you really mean it! If necessary, explain that this behaviour could be classified as sexual harassment and you expect it to stop immediately. Keep a written record of occasions when harassment occurs and of what was said when you objected. The record should include dates, times and names of witnesses, etc.

2. If the harassment occurs again, repeat your earlier objections. Back them up with a written letter or email.

Refer to your earlier spoken complaint. State only the facts. Make *at least three copies* of this information. Send one copy to the offending person and one to his or her supervisor. Keep one copy for your records. (Additional copies may be sent to your own supervisor and the chief executive officer of your company if you think it's appropriate.)

3. If the behaviour continues, or if the company or union fails to deal with it, lodge a formal complaint with your regional branch of the Anti-discrimination Commission of your State or Territory. When in doubt, call the government body and ask to talk to a trained counsellor. If the situation is serious enough, involve the police by lodging a sexual assault charge.

Note: If the first incident is serious enough, state your complaint *orally* and in writing (with copies to applicable parties) and lodge a formal complaint with the government body.

Most human rights codes now specify that the person responsible for the act of sexual harassment, plus supervisors, managers, or people in positions of authority who are aware of the sexual harassment and do not take immediate and appropriate action, plus the company in question, may all be named in a complaint brought before the government body.

No longer can others in positions of power look the other way and ignore the fact that sexual harassment is occurring. A supervisor who does nothing about the sexual harassment of an employee is regarded as having condoned the harassment. If the employee knows that the supervisor has observed or is aware of the situation, s/he can include the supervisor in the charge of sexual harassment. Companies should have formal sexual harassment policies posted where all employees can see them.

Workplace Bullying

Society assumes that in a bullying situation, there is a male aggressor and a female victim, but females can be as vicious as males. Female bullies are more spiteful, devious, manipulative and vengeful. These individuals use gossip and backstabbing to undermine, discredit or devalue others' contributions. They have poorly defined moral and ethical boundaries and put others down to make themselves feel important.

Bullying includes:

- Being belittled, demeaned or patronised - especially in front of others;

- Being disgraced, shouted at and threatened, often in front of others;

- Making snide comments to see if the person will fight back;

- Finding fault and criticising everything the victim says and does or twisting, distorting and misrepresenting the victim. The criticism can be of a trivial nature and often there's a grain of truth in the criticism, so it can dupe the victim into believing the criticism is valid;

- An unvarying refusal to recognise the victim's contributions;

- Attempting to chip away at the person's status, self-confidence, worth and potential;

- Treating them differently - showing favouritism to others and bias towards the victim.

Workplace bullying is the deliberate, repeated and hurtful mistreatment of one person by another. Others refer to it as harassment, emotional abuse, targeted aggression or abuse of power that undermines self-confidence and causes stress. It's constant, inappropriate, overt and covert behaviour that criticizes, belittles, isolates and undermines the victim. It involves humiliation, sabotage, spreading gossip, overwork, unnecessary pressure, delaying tactics and it can escalate into physical and verbal assault, sexual assault and even arson. Evidence shows that bullying is normally repeated and can escalate in intensity over time.

What do some say about workplace bullying? They identify it as people being *"too sensitive,"* or it's a *"personality conflict"* or *"poor interpersonal relationships"* - but bullying - they can't see it that way. ***Well, it IS bullying.***

Who are the Bullies?

Until recently, psychologically violent people in the workplace were regarded as tough managers or difficult people, or at worst a *"pain in the neck."* These attitudes are changing as the dysfunction, inefficiency, cost and severe psychiatric injury caused by these people's behaviour is revealed.

An employee's worst nightmare may be that their bully is their direct supervisor. Typically, bullying comes from a boss to a subordinate in the form of verbal or emotional abuse. It includes yelling, swearing or ridiculing, continual and trivial fault-finding, chronic unjustified criticism, berating, intimidation, public humiliation or sabotaging of achievements. Or they set an employee up to fail by overloading them with work, inconsistently and unjustifiably changing work responsibilities and even cancelling holiday schedules.

But the workplace bully can also be a co-worker who may be a silent snake-in-the-grass - who cruelly bullies through manipulation, isolation, exclusion and gossip.

Ways of Bullying

Physical Bullies:

They act out their anger in physical ways. They resort to hitting or kicking their victims or damaging the victim's property. Of all the types of bullies, this one is easiest to identify, because his or her behaviour is so obvious. This is the type of bully our imagination conjures up when we try to picture a bully. They are well known in their environment. As they get older, physical bullies can become more aggressive in their attacks. Once they become adults this aggressive attitude is well ingrained in the bully's personality.

Verbal Bullies:

It's quite difficult for a victim to ignore this type of bully. They use words that hurt and humiliate their victims, resorting to name-calling, insulting, making racist comments and teasing. While this type of bullying doesn't result in physical scars, its emotional effects can be devastating. It's the easiest form of attack for a bully. It's quick and painless for the bully, but often remarkably harmful for the victim.

Mob or Group Bullies:

These are predominantly female bullies who exclude their victims from feeling part of a group. They exploit the feeling of insecurity in their victims. They ambush their victims by convincing peers to exclude or reject the victim. They often use the same tricks that a verbal bully uses with his/her victims to isolate them. Spreading nasty rumours about the victim is part of the pattern. It can be an extremely harmful form of bullying because it excludes the victim from his or her peer group.

Mobbing is ganging up on someone that causes psychic terror. It's routine in chickens where a formal pecking order is seen. The bird at the bottom of the pecking order often dies from the effects of being shunned, kept from food and water and physically picked on by the rest of the brood.

Who are the targets of bullies?

It's often assumed that victims of bullying are weak, inadequate and are loners, but most are independent, self-reliant and aren't interested in office politics. Bullies select individuals who prefer to use dialogue to resolve conflict. The victims have a low propensity for violence and will go to great lengths to avoid conflict. They constantly try to use negotiation rather than resort to grievance and legal action. Targets are chosen because they're competent and popular. Bullies are jealous of the easy and stable relationships that targets have with others.

How to prevent and stop Workplace Bullying

Only specific legislation can protect workers. Many fall short of the mark, by insisting that bullying must be ongoing. To the victim - one incident of bullying can be enough and should have all the protection of the law to deal with it. It's been proven that no amount of *"Codes of Conduct"* or *"Guidance Notes"* will do this. Legislation often does not cover most situations where a bully makes another worker's life a living hell.

It's the responsibility of every company to provide a workplace that's a safe and healthy place to work in. There needs to be a corporate responsibility to deal with the bullying behaviour and recognise the signs of a toxic workplace. Executives can show they care about employees by providing an environment free of harassment of any kind - not just lip service - but demonstrated by their own behaviour. Senior executives must not ignore bullying episodes. Unfortunately, many senior executives also bully their staff. They need to examine their company vision and see that *every* employee (including themselves) follows that vision.

CHAPTER EIGHT

SUPERVISORS WHO LACK SUPERVISORY SKILLS

Many supervisors, unfortunately, have had little or no supervisory training. Everyone benefits from this kind of training. Even if supervisors need to pay for the training themselves, it's one of the best investments they can make towards their future success.

Supervisors who lack supervisory training can be very frustrating to work for. They may not know how to delegate, how to discipline subordinates, or how to motivate different types of employees. Or, in various ways, they may make it difficult for their staff to operate efficiently. If your supervisor is one of these, you may have to take active steps and suggest the company provide him or her with supervisory training.

Poor delegation

"My boss is great with people but is vague at times on how he wants me to do things. He gives unclear directions, then changes his mind the next day."

You'll succeed with this type of boss, if you fill in the details of any work he delegates to you. Use paraphrasing to make sure that what he originally says is what you hear. If there are any unclear areas, ask questions about what he wants. If he's in the habit of changing his mind the next day, write down the instructions, show the list to him, and confirm his instructions.

Later, show your confusion when he changes his instructions and bring out your list of instructions made earlier. Update the instructions as requested. Soon your supervisor will realise how often he changes his instructions. He may learn to take more time when formulating his requests. This person would probably benefit greatly by attending a time-management course. This would teach him to save time by planning before delegating tasks to subordinates.

Sometimes supervisors are disorganised. They're the ones who explain that they know where everything is on their messy desks. They hate details. This boss hates bad news, so stress what you're going to do about things rather than dwell on the problem.

"My boss asks me to do things that really aren't my job."

Use paraphrasing to make sure you understand what your supervisor expects from you. Have your job description updated. Then talk with your supervisor to see if someone else can handle the duty that you feel doesn't fit your position.

Perfectionist

"My boss is a perfectionist who sometimes expects too much from his staff."

Anticipate your boss's needs. Don't skip details and double-check each assignment before handing it in. Give alternatives. Have plans B and C available, should they be necessary. Submit new ideas in writing, including the pros and cons and the alternatives available.

Poor Disciplinary Skills

"My boss disciplines me in public."

This is a major *faux pas* on the part of your supervisor. Your first attempt should be to make the person understand and empathize with your feelings. Using the technique of feedback to let the supervisor know how humiliating it is when s/he disciplines you in front of others. Explain that you could accept criticism far more easily if it were given privately. You might have to add that if you are publicly disciplined in future, you'll simply walk away.

Wants us to compete

"My boss is a very competition-oriented person. He wants me to compete with co-workers and I don't want to."

You may be in the wrong profession. Competing against other employees is the most popular system management uses to encourage staff to make more sales.

Many people respond much better to the challenge of beating their own sales records than to competition with others.

Companies should ensure that the standards of competition are fair to those at all levels of experience. If you're new with the company, you can't be expected to compete with someone with an established territory and clientele. Trainees with six months experience should compete against others in the company with the same experience. Many in sales enjoy competition. Others don't but are encouraged to set realistic objectives for themselves.

Many sales supervisors can be very stressful to work for. They expect assertive or aggressive behaviour from their staff. Pushover behaviour is not acceptable. You need to prepare carefully to discuss a problem with such a boss. Be sure you have several workable solutions to suggest before attempting to negotiate changes.

Won't defend me

"My boss doesn't back me up when I get into trouble with clients. She always takes the client's side, and I end up defending myself, even though I'm in the right."

Supervisors who automatically take the client's side in a client-employee dispute are doing their subordinates a grave injustice. Until the employee has had a chance to explain his or her side of the story, the supervisor should remain neutral.

The supervisor should record all the facts given by the client and assure the client that the matter will be investigated.

If your supervisor fails to back you up when you know you're carrying out your duties correctly, use the feedback technique to explain how you feel about being unjustly blamed.

Say, *"I have a problem and I need your help in solving it. Last week a client wanted me to bend the rules for her. I explained to her that I had strict guidelines I was expected to follow and said I couldn't do what she wanted. She then spoke to you and got her way. This same thing has happened with four clients in the past month. I felt foolish when she came by my office to tell me she had got what she wanted. I'm wondering if the rules have changed and how I'm to deal with these kinds of problems in the future."*

Does not give me credit for my contributions

I've heard both men and women say (and we'll assume the boss is a men), *"I worked all week on that report, and my boss took full credit for it. That's the last time he's going to do that to me!"*

When your supervisor *"steals"* your ideas and takes credit for them, you've made him look good. He needs you to do this. If you don't let him take the credit, he'll hold you back.

For instance, if you write a new policy-and-procedures manual for your department, you supervisor can take full credit for its contents. He has the right (according to the existing unwritten rules of business) to use your ideas and do it with a clear conscience. According to business rules, you (the subordinate) are there to make your supervisor or manager look good. Therefore, your ideas become your supervisor's ideas, and the supervisor is not breaking any rules by taking the credit. Most men and women dislike this rule. Many supervisors don't feel that they're doing anything wrong, because *"everybody does it"*.

I disagree completely with this business practice and encourage supervisors to give credit where credit's due. Supervisors who keep stealing their subordinates' ideas only de-motivate them. Chances are, they'll get bad suggestions or no suggestions at all from their staff in future. If a subordinate has come up with a new method of making a widget, that employee should get the praise and recognition, not the supervisor. What does it matter if the subordinate gets the credit for the good idea? The supervisor could submit the report under his or her name but give credit to the subordinates who helped prepare the report.

If your supervisor is an old-style limelight-stealer and you can't get along with it, send your new ideas or suggestions to him or her in the form of an email. Ask for your supervisor's opinion about the merit of your idea. Then it's in writing. Or offer your suggestions at a meeting where others know that it's *your* idea.

"I have to do my boss's work in an acting capacity without extra pay. When he's away, I must handle his job as well as my own. I don't think this is fair."

Try using the feedback technique to explain your problem. If that doesn't work, look upon the experience as a developmental phase of your employment. Ask your supervisor which duties you can let slide during this double-duty period.

It looks excellent on a resume when you're able to add *"acting supervisory duties while supervisor away."* This statement may help you get future supervisory positions. So, take the extra work anyway, if you think you can manage to handle two jobs for short periods.

Interferes with my supervision

Dennis had a problem with his manager, Jim. Dennis was new in his position as supervisor of a staff of four. Under the guise of *"helping"* him, Jim allowed Dennis's staff to bypass Dennis to obtain help directly from him.

Jim was breaking one of the cardinal rules in business by undermining the control and authority Dennis needed to supervisor his staff properly. There's a strict rule in business regarding the line of command; managers are not supposed to bypass the supervisor to give work directly to the supervisor's subordinates. Nor should managers get involved in matters of discipline or in performance appraisals that concern the supervisor's staff. Dennis was advised to use the feedback technique to explain that his group's effectiveness was undermined when he had only partial control over his subordinates' work. He should remind Jim that he, Dennis is ultimately responsible for everything he and his staff do and that he needs full control to do his job effectively.

Is unavailable to staff and clients

Shirley asked how she could get her supervisor to tell her where he was. There was an in-out board, but he seldom used it and often left by the back door. He was seldom available: was in meetings, out of the office, or sitting behind a closed door.

Shirley was advised to itemise occasions when she had been forced to handle problems on her own and give her supervisor a list of the difficulties that arose because he wasn't available for consultation. She should then ask her supervisor if there is an alternative supervisor she could consult when he can't be reached. She would also ask if he would give her the authority (in writing) to handle such situations when he was not available.

Does not respect privacy

"My supervisor wants to know all about my personal life, and I don't want to talk about it."

Say, *"I prefer to keep a clear division between my private and business life. I've found it's better for me."* If your supervisor pushes further, ask, *"Why is my private life so important to you?"* The supervisor is thus forced to account for his or her aggressive behaviour.

Does not provide opportunities for advancement

Andrew felt frustrated because his supervisor refused to give him assignments that would prepare him for his next promotional opportunity. His title was Buyer 1 (the first step on the ladder for the purchasing manager's position). His supervisor, Mel, had been in the Buyer 2 position for five years. He refused to allow Andrew to learn anything relating to a future promotion.

In this situation, Mel felt that Andrew was a *"heel-nipper"* (someone after his supervisory job), while Andrew felt that Mel was *"locked into"* his position and threatened by Andrew's promotional expectations.

Mel didn't understand that his reluctance to prepare Andrew for his position was why he wasn't moving ahead in the company. Often, supervisors who have no one ready to take over their position will themselves be overlooked for a promotion. Andrew was advised to bring this information to

Mel's attention. If that didn't work, he could take a lateral move into a position comparable to his existing one, or try for a promotion in another department

He was initially reluctant to move to another department because such a move represented a detour from the direct route to the purchasing manager's position. When I explained that this might be the only way he could bypass Mel's position, he agreed to try it. He's now the Purchasing Manager and supervises Mel.

Check your own attitude

An important factor affecting your dealings with your supervisor is your own attitude to supervision. Even the best employees sometimes need guidance and even correction from their supervisor. It is true that there are difficult supervisors who habitually give the necessary guidance in negative form, as criticism. But there are also employees who are too ready to perceive legitimate correction as criticism.

The art of being supervised consists of being able to accept suggestions that will help you improve your performance. Whether these suggestions come to you in the harsh form of criticism or in the milder form of correction or instruction, you need to learn how to handle them in a positive way. The following steps may help you in your effort to learn the delicate art of being supervised.

Dealing with Criticism

When your supervisor corrects or criticises you:

1. Control your thoughts and behaviour. Keep in mind that there may be some truth in the criticism (you'll miss it if you concentrate only on how you can defend yourself).

2. Don't respond angrily. Instead, listen carefully to the comments.

3. Ask for specifics if the criticism is vague. For example, if your supervisor says, *"I don't like your attitude,"* ask, *"What is it about my attitude that concerns you?"* Your supervisor might respond with, *"Well, you were rude to*

that client when you served her a few minutes ago. You kept her waiting far too long before you looked after her." You may not like what you hear, but at least you have something specific to deal with.

4. Use the technique of paraphrasing to confirm your understanding of the problem.

5. If the criticism is valid, apologise and let your supervisor know what steps you'll take to correct the behaviour or the problem. Leave guilt trips behind. Don't let the criticism overwhelm you and affect the rest of your day; instead, simply decide that you won't make the same mistake again.

6. Above all, don't climb into a shell, work to rule or give poor performance if you are criticised for something. We often set up this kind of defence mechanism in ourselves. If we feel that something or someone hurts us (especially a supervisor), we're likely to back off and *"lick our wounds."*

CHAPTER NINE
DEALING WITH CO-WORKERS

In a sense, everyone employed by your company is your co-worker, but for the purposes of this chapter, co-worker refers to employees whose behaviour in the workplace affects you, but with whom you have no direct reporting relationship (they do not supervisor you; you do not supervise them). Dealing with this kind of co-worker can be tricky, because if you try to get them to change their behaviour and don't handle it just right, they may think you're trying to boss them. And bossing co-workers when you're not their supervisor is, of course a classic workplace no-no. Co-workers' behaviour that may bother you can take a variety of forms.

Unprofessional Behaviour

Most employees want to do a good job, and to be important to their companies. People who are committed to doing the best job possible, set high standards for their own job performance and earn the right to be very proud of their work. Their consistently professional behaviour also brings them the trust and respect of supervisors, clients and co-workers.

The professionalism of your colleagues will, to a large extent, determine whether your work place is congenial or not. In most workplaces, people's jobs are independent, and each worker's effectiveness and productivity are usually tied in some way to how well others perform their roles in the company. The unprofessional behaviour of one employee can affect the efficiency of many. Although most of us would prefer to live and let live, when co-worker's inefficiency interferes with our own performance, it is useful to know what sort of action can be taken to correct the problem.

Don't do their share of the work

Do you have co-workers who don't do their share of the work, but receive more than their share of salary? If you feel this is true, discuss it with your boss. Companies that implement a *"merit system"* seldom face this problem.

People may use a variety of tactics to avoid their responsibilities. Being habitually late and being away from their desks are two of the commonest ploys.

People don't like to be kept waiting! They feel that their time is important - and object to being treated as if it isn't.

"I have a friend who I often have lunch with or attend meetings with, but she's always late. Besides using feedback, what else can I do to solve this situation?"

Let her know what the consequences will be should she keep you waiting the next time. Tell her that if she isn't ready when you come for her, you'll leave without her. Then do it! If you are to meet her for lunch, wait only ten minutes before ordering your meal.

George works on a front desk of a government office and deals directly with the public. Walter, a co-worker, is often late for work. This makes George's job twice as busy, because he needs to cover the desk by himself.

Using feedback, he said, *"Walter, you probably don't realise the double-workload I have every time you're late. This makes our department look bad. What do you think you can do to stop this from happening in the future?"* (Note that George focused on the consequences for the department, not any personal grievance he felt.)

a) The problem - George has a double workload when Walter is late for work.

b) His feelings or reactions - *"This makes our department look bad."*

c) The solution - George asked Walter to solve the problem.

Betty is a receptionist. One of her duties is to answer the phone for her department. They have in-out boards that all members of the staff are supposed to keep up to date. Unfortunately, one employee, Mildred leaves her desk, and even the office, without letting Betty know where to find her. Nor does Mildred have another staff member answer her phone for her when she can't. When clients ask for Mildred, Betty puts the caller through to her desk. If Mildred doesn't answer her after the first few rings, the call is returned to her.

Betty said she felt like a fool when she had to explain that she didn't know where Mildred was, or when she would return.

Using feedback, she started her conversation with Mildred by saying, *"I have a problem and I need your help in solving it."* Then she asked Mildred what she would suggest that would stop the problem from recurring. (This dumps the problem into Mildred's lap where it belongs.) Mildred still shrugged it off, so Betty added, *"I need your co-operation, so I can do my job properly for the company. It must appear stupid to the client when I must admit that I don't know where you are. Can't we find some solution that will be acceptable to both of us?"*

Betty's persistence eventually produced a compromise that was acceptable to both women. Mildred agreed that she would let Betty know where she was. She arranged for a co-worker to answer her phone when she was away from her desk.

Pass the Buck

Buck-passers are co-workers who shift their work onto the desks of other people. They do this by defining their own responsibilities as narrowly as possible. They are adept at determining why certain tasks are someone else's responsibility.

Shirley reported the following problem: *"The woman on the switchboard seems to transfer calls to me when she isn't sure whom the caller should be talking to. I'm too busy with my own work to do part of her work too."*

Shirley should first check her job description to see if that task is part of her assigned duties. If not, she should talk to her boss. She would start the conversation, *"I have a problem and I need your help in solving it. Sally, on switchboard, is transferring calls to me when she isn't sure whom the caller should be talking to. Am I supposed to do this, or should I suggest she put the calls through to someone else?"* This will allow her boss to know what's going on, and to decide what s/he wants Shirley to do about the problem.

Other buck-passers refuse to admit their mistake. They say, *"Who me? I didn't do that!"* when they know they're at fault.

Deal with this by obtaining as much information as you can to prove that the person did do what they did. Again, talk to your supervisor about your concerns over co-worker's failure to take responsibility for his/her mistakes. Explain that you know anyone can make a mistake, but that it hurts you and other staff if co-workers try to pretend their errors are someone else's fault.

Procrastinates

Here are five major types of procrastinators:

1. *Hurry-up type.* They wait until the last minute and work around the clock to meet deadlines.

2. *I'll decide tomorrow.* They postpone decisions until events resolve the situation or a decision is forced on them.

3. *Perfectionists.* They must complete all tasks faultlessly, no matter how insignificant. (These people need to learn to discriminate between important and unimportant assignments.)

4. *I'll show 'em.* They delay completing assignments as a way of retaining a sense of personal power and control. This normally happens when they're delegated a task they don't want to do or feel someone else should do.

5. *Muddler.* They put off work because of bad habits, poor organization or lack of set procedures. They may go in circles, getting less and less accomplished as time goes on. These people start something but leave it for another task before completing the original one.

Aggressive behaviour

The suggestions in earlier chapters on dealing with aggressive behaviour of supervisors will be useful for resolving problems of this type of co-worker. An assertive response is usually the best course of action.

Over-achievers or competitive types

If some of your co-workers are over-achievers who try to make you feel inadequate, do the best you can. Don't let a co-worker try to set standards for you. Performance standards with your company should be based on average performance, not high or an over-achiever's performance. Speak to your supervisor if you feel the standards of performance are unfair.

Here's an example:

Jill had trouble with a co-worker, Sue, who was forever competing with her, even in the most trivial things. For instance, Sue kept challenging Jill to take a typing test with her to see who could type faster. Jill had done this on her noon hour twice already, and found she typed 65 w.p.m. with two errors. Sue typed 80 w.p.m. with eight errors, and felt she was a better typist. Sue spent much of her time at work correcting her errors. Jill objected when Sue called her a poor sport because she refused to do a third test.

Jill used the feedback technique to let Sue know how she felt about Sue's competitive approach to things. *"Sue, it's not important to me who's the better typist, but I am getting upset because you keep insisting that I compete with you. Why do you feel you always have to be the best in everything you do?"*

"I like to win."

"Have you ever considered what others might be feeling when you try to force them to compete?"

"Everybody competes."

"Have you checked this out with others?"

"No, I haven't"

"Then maybe you should. I, for one, don't want to compete with others. If I'm doing the best job I can, I don't have to know I'm better than others."

Sue didn't concede completely but thought more about her competitive approach to life. She saved competing for situations that warranted its use. Because she worked in the sales department of her firm, she was able to channel her competitiveness against other companies instead of against her co-workers.

Hyper-critical

When others (especially those whom you don't give a hoot about) criticise you unfairly, try the following: calmly acknowledge to your critic, that there *may* be some truth in what s/he says. This allows you to receive criticism comfortably, without becoming anxious or defensive, and gives no reward to those using the manipulative criticism. For example:

- **Agree with some aspect of the comment that is true.**

  "You're wearing that awful blouse today."
  "That's right, I am wearing this blouse."

- **Agree that the comment may possibly have some validity**

  "You're not very careful."
  "Maybe I'm not very careful."

- **Agree with the logic of the comment**

  "If we bought a new truck now instead of keeping the old clunker, we'd be a lot safer on the road and wouldn't have these high repair bills."
  "You're right. A new truck would have those advantages."
  (Rather than, *"There you go, another way to spend our money."*)

- **Allow for improvement**

  "Your dresses don't fit you correctly."
  "I'm sure they could fit better."

- **Show empathy**

  "You're being very unfair."
  "I can see that you feel I'm unfair."

Keeps interrupting my work

Not all interruptions or interrupters are unjustified. A certain number of interruptions are part of any job, and no one expects co-workers to refrain altogether from social exchanges. It's when interruptions get out of hand, that action is needed.

First, keep a log to determine who causes your interruptions, when, and for how long. You may find that a large portion of your day is spent dealing with interruptions. If you feel that they are keeping you from doing your *"real"* work, you may need to change your attitude. Perhaps dealing with these so-called interruptions is really an important part of your job, as importing as completing reports. If that's the case, you need to respond by telling yourself *"That's my job calling!"*

If, however, your log reveals that many interruptions are not job-related, you need to analyse your findings more closely. Some of these interruptions may be your fault, in the sense that you may appear willing to be interrupted or may be reluctant to tell people you're too busy to talk to them. In this case you need to change your own behaviour.

Try doing the following:

- If people just want to chat, suggest they catch you during coffee break.
- Set time limits for meetings and stick to them.
- Whenever possible meet people in their offices, so you can leave when you want to.

One of Debbie's co-workers used to ignore the fact that Debbie was on the phone and start talking to her. Debbie found it impossible to concentrate properly on her caller because of her co-worker's distracting behaviour.

Debbie could have handed her co-worker a piece of paper and a pen, indicating that she could leave a written message. Later, using feedback. Debbie could explain to her co-worker the difficulties caused by her behaviour.

Personality Conflicts

Sometimes the chemistry between you and a co-worker is just wrong. Normally you would just avoid such a person, but personality conflicts can be serious if your job requires you to work together.

"I don't get along with my co-worker, and my boss won't do anything about the situation. We're at each other's throats all the time."

The first thing you could do is try to get the other employee to talk to you about the problem. You could start by saying, *"Jim, we're always at each other's throats. This is affecting our productivity and both our chances for advancement in this company. Can you think of anything we can do to stop the problem we're having?"*

If the initial attempt fails, you should then approach your supervisor directly. Start by saying, *"I have a problem and I need your help in solving it. Jim and I seem to be on different wavelengths, and we're always at each other's throats. I've tried to resolve our differences, but it doesn't seem to have worked. Can you suggest anything I can do to help us get along better and be more productive?"* If the conflict really is affecting your and Jim's productivity, your supervisor needs to be aware of it. It then becomes the supervisor's responsibility to resolve the problem.

Conducting effective meetings

Methods of chairing meetings differ slightly from those for dealing generally with co-workers, because the position of chair gives you some authority over the other participants. However, although the chair has certain powers that other members of the group do not, it is widely agreed that the most successful chairs do not *"boss"* the meeting. Their job is to:

(a) make it possible for all participants to contribute their expertise, and

(b) ensure that the purpose of the meeting is accomplished within the allotted time.

If you've ever headed a meeting, you know just how difficult it is to do both these things simultaneously. You want to move things along without missing a valuable contribution. You want to encourage contributions while controlling people who threaten to *"take over"* the meeting.

There are a variety of techniques that are helpful for dealing with the special problems of meetings. For instance, if someone's too talkative, you can interrupt with, *"That's an interesting point. What do the rest of you think about this?"* or, *"We've been making Byron do all the work. What do the rest of you think about this?"*

If the meeting's in progress and tempers flare, it's the chair's job to emphasize points of agreement and minimise points of disagreement. You can draw attention to the objectives of the meeting or ask direct questions relating to the topic. Or you could invite a contribution from a participant whom you know to be good at resolving disputes: *"What do you think, Alex?"*

Even *before* a meeting starts, if you suspect that there will be personality conflicts, talk to those involved before going to the meeting. Ask them to leave their negative attitudes towards each other out of the meeting room.

For instance, let's say you're a team leader for a project where several of your co-workers need to work together in harmony to get the job done. You know that Bill and Jim dislike each other because they had a heated argument at the last meeting and one of them stormed out. Before the next meeting you might say, *"Bill, I've decided to talk to you before the meeting. I'm going to talk to Jim as well. I expect the two of you to participate fully at this meeting and you won't be able to do so if you get upset with each other. Can I count on you to cooperate?"*

If you see any reluctance or resistance, you may have to add: *"If we have a repeat performance of last week's meeting, I'll have to speak to your manager, so we can get this project completed."*

Here are some tips to enable you to handle the range of difficult participants you could encounter at a meeting:

Dealing with problem participants at meetings

Participant is: Overly talkative - to the extent that other participants do not have an opportunity to contribute.

Participant may be: An *"eager beaver;"* exceptionally well informed; naturally wordy; nervous.

What to do: Interrupt with *"That's an interesting point… Let's see what everyone else thinks."* Directly call on others. Suggest *"Let's put others to work."* When the person stops for a breath, thank him or her, restate the pertinent points and move on.

Participant is: Engaging in side conversations with others in the group.

Participant may be: Talking about something related to the discussion; discussing a personal matter; uninterested in the topic under discussion.

What to do: Direct a question to the person. Restate the last idea or suggestion expressed by the group and ask for the person's opinion.

Participant is: Argumentative – to the extent that others' ideas or opinions are rejected, or others are treated unfairly.

Participant may be: Seriously upset about the issue under discussion; upset by personal or job problems; intolerant of others; lacking in empathy; a negative thinker.

What to do: Keep your temper in check. Try to find some merit in what's said; get the group to see it too, then move on to something else. Talk to the person privately and point out what his or her actions are doing to the rest of the group. Try to gain the person's cooperation. Encourage the person to concentrate on positives, not negatives.

Participant is: Unable to express self so that everyone understands.

Participant may be: Nervous, shy, excited; Not used to participating in discussions

What to do: Rephrase, restating what the person said, asking for confirmation of accuracy. Allow the person ample time to express his or herself. Help the person along without being condescending.

Participant is: Always seeking approval.

Participant may be: Looking for advice; trying to get leader to support his or her point of view; trying to put leader on the spot.

What to do: Avoid taking sides, especially if the group will be unduly influenced by your point of view.

Participant is: Bickering with another participant.

Participant may be: Carrying on an old grudge; feeling very strongly about the issue.

What to do: Emphasise points of agreement, minimise points of disagreement. Direct participants' attention to the objectives of the meeting. Mention time limits of the meeting. Ask participants to shelve the issue for the moment.

Participant is: Too quiet, unwilling to contribute.

Participant may be: Bored, indifferent, timid, insecure; more knowledgeable or experienced than the rest of the group.

What to do: Direct questions to the person that you're confident s/he can respond to. Capitalise on the person's knowledge or experience by using them as a resource person.

Participant is: Seeking attention.

Participant may be: Feeling inferior; Hiding a lack of knowledge by clowning around.

What to do: Keep reminding the person about the topic being discussed. Talk to the person privately. Point out what his or her actions are doing to the rest of the group.

Participant is: Uninvolved and unwilling to commit to new tasks.

Participant may be: Lazy; too busy already; feeling s/he should not have been asked to the meeting in the first place.

What to do: Ask for facts concerning the person's schedule. Ask the person to volunteer for tasks (others in group must as well). Make sure you ask the right people to future meetings.

Participant is: Already too over-committed to other things to take on new tasks.

Participant may be: Unaware of own skills and abilities; lacking in organisational skills.

What to do: Ask for facts concerning the person's schedule. Ask the person whether s/he is already over-committed. Tell the person you're counting on him or her. Send the person to a time-management seminar.

Participant is: A buck-passer who blames others for anything negative that happens and doesn't accept new tasks readily.

Participant may be: Unable to admit to making mistakes; Afraid to take risks.

What to do: Make the person account for his or her actions. Ask for facts to back up allegations. Privately ask why the person won't accept new tasks.

Suppose that you chair a meeting and delegate project assignments to a group. What do you do when you have a follow-up meeting and get these lame excuses?

   a. *"I didn't know I was responsible for that!"*

   b. *"I didn't agree to do that!"*

   c *"I thought you didn't need that till next week."*

The follow-through techniques below may help you ensure that participants follow through too.

1. Set an agenda with time limits (give it to them before the meeting). Then follow the agenda.

2. During the meeting, delegate responsibility as required.

3. Set firm time deadlines for each commitment.

4. At the end of the meeting, ask everyone to confirm that s/he understands the task. *"What is it you have to do before our meeting on December 10th? Sam...? Sally...? Bronwyn...?"*

5. Follow up with written information (meeting notes).

CHAPTER TEN
DEALING WITH SUBORDINATES

Understanding the supervisory role

There are five essential elements to a supervisor's role. The person with full supervisory status has the responsibility for:

Delegating work;

Checking work;

Conducting performance appraisals;

Disciplining subordinates;

Hiring his or her own staff.

1. ***Delegating work.*** This involves giving tasks to your subordinates for completion.

2. ***Checking work.*** This is done to see that employees complete their tasks properly. You'll check the quantity and quality of the work performed and how long it took to complete.

3. ***Conducting performance appraisals.*** You and nobody else should have the responsibility for doing performance appraisals for all your subordinates. Your manager shouldn't do them, because s/he is not directly responsible for the work of your subordinates. Your manager might review your findings to see if they're fair, but you complete the appraisal on each employee you supervise

4. ***Disciplining subordinates.*** Because your staff ends up making you look either good or bad, you need this control to correct production and/or behaviour problems. However, because of the potential dangers of *"wrongful dismissal"* suits, many companies arrange for the actual firing of employees to be handled by those specially trained in its implementation.

5. ***Hiring staff.*** If possible, have as much input as you can into the hiring of people who work for you. If you're on different wavelengths, it can be difficult for you and your staff to work as a team.

Unfortunately, most employment interviewers decide whether they will hire a person within the first four minutes of the interview. They base their decision on what they see, hear and believe. They're evaluating the person's non-verbal language - how they walk, talk, sit and shake hands - and their verbal communication skills - how well they express themselves, their self-esteem level, etc.

At this point in the interview, the interviewers haven't even begun to ask the questions that should be the determiners of whether they hire the person or not

If you have the responsibility of hiring staff, keep an open mind until the end of the interview. This way, your decision is based on more concrete information.

How does your supervisory position measure up? If you have only the first two responsibilities, you're in a *"lead hand"* position. I believe that all lead hand positions should be abolished because this is a no-win situation for them. If they don't have the responsibility to conduct performance appraisals and discipline staff, they'll receive only token respect from their subordinates and will have little control over the outcome of their work.

If you don't have that control over your employees and they do an unsatisfactory job, who looks bad? You do! If your company puts you in this position, talk to your manager and ask that you have the first four responsibilities (and the fifth, if possible). If your request is refused, ask that the manager look after the delegation and checking of responsibilities as well, and explain your reasons.

Supervising former peers

How should you handle the first day on the job where you're suddenly responsible for supervising your former peers? You'll likely fail if you don't handle that first day or week properly. It's necessary to remove any feelings of envy and jealousy your new subordinates might have.

Your manager will usually call a meeting to introduce you to your new staff, then leave so you can take over the meeting.

If you anticipate hard feelings, deal with your former co-workers' feelings first. Start by saying, *"I know a few of you applied for and wanted this promotion. I can understand that you may feel a little upset that I got the position instead of you. The company chose me, so what we do from now on depends on how all of us work together. I need your support to handle my job properly. In return, I'll do everything I can to be a good supervisor. Can I count on you for your support?"*

Ask those present, one by one, to indicate to you whether you can rely on them: *"Margie - how about you, can I count on your support?"* *"Dave?"* Cover every employee in the room. If your staff have made a verbal commitment to you, they're much more likely to cooperate in the future.

If you detect reluctance to make the commitment, don't let it pass. In a private interview, say, *"Margie, I detect some hesitancy in your reply. What can I do to make the situation a little easier for you?"*

If she still balks, you'll have to keep your eye on her. She might try to sabotage your efforts. If she does, you'll have to be on top of the situation and implement immediate disciplinary action. Don't be afraid to do it. Nip the problem in the bud; don't let it grow and flourish and contaminate the others in your section.

Delegating

Many supervisors fail because they lack the ability to delegate tasks properly to their staff. They make excuses such as:

- *"I need this completed right now. I could finish this job and three others if I did it myself. It would take twice as long to train someone else, then check to see they did it right!"*

- *"This job is so important that only I can do it."*

- *"I'm afraid my staff will fail."*

- *"I can do this better than anyone else."*

- *"I don't want my people to think I'm a tyrant."*

Many hidden reasons are behind the above explanations. Supervisors don't delegate enough tasks because:

- They fear a loss of control. It reflects directly on them if their staff makes mistakes.

- They fear losing their jobs. Some supervisors feel that if they delegate too much, they'll have no job left to do. Another expression is, *"Suppose someone on my staff becomes better than me?"*

Many supervisors are unaware of an important factor in delegation. Failure to groom staff to succeed them could result in their being overlooked themselves when a more responsible position is being filled. Proving that there is someone ready to take over their existing position is one way of showing management they're eligible for promotion. (One way to prove this is to ensure there's at least one employee who can be placed in an acting position when the supervisor is away.)

Motivating Employees

Of course, much more is involved in supervision than simply assigning and checking work, assessing performance and disciplining employees. Supervising people is an art that depends on how well you can motivate people.

Supervisors must watch for the *"Pygmalion effect"* when trying to motivate staff. If a supervisor believes employees are smart, s/he will treat them that way. If a supervisor believes employees are capable of independent thought, s/he will also treat them that way. However, unfortunately, if the supervisor believes that they are lazy, stupid or slow to pick up new ideas (or have any other undesirable attributes), s/he will often treat them that way too. People respond to what they perceive is wanted from them. If supervisors expect high achievement, that's also likely what they'll get. If supervisors expect low productivity, that's likely what they'll get.

Do you need to change your attitude towards the abilities of your staff? Are you letting the Pygmalion effect influence how you supervise your staff?

Some people are motivated by their interest in the work itself. Other motivators are the desire or need for:

- Money
- Acceptance by peers
- Competition/challenge
- Awards
- Status
- Better working conditions
- Job security
- Promotional opportunities
- A better office
- Extra benefits
- Recognition for good work.

It's possible that your employees only hear from you when they've made mistakes. It's normal for all of us to want to receive praise and recognition for work well done. It's the best motivator of all. Give it a try. See if things don't change.

Be aware that it's not possible to motivate everyone - you just *can't* motivate some people. With unsatisfactory workers, start by spelling out exactly what you expect of them (document your requests properly). Then give them ample opportunity to improve their performance. If they refuse to conform, replace them with good workers. There are too many excellent people who are unemployed for companies to keep foot-draggers on the payroll. They just de-motivate everyone around them.

Acquaint yourself with some of the standard procedures for managing human resources and try to get your company to use them, if it is not already doing so. Such basic tools of personnel management as job descriptions and performance appraisals help employees feel that they know what is expected of them and that their efforts are recognised. They can be confident that procedures are in place to allow them to develop their skills and earn promotions. The advantages of some of these management tools are discussed in the examples that follow.

Staff Problems

Giving credit for contributions

"My staff expect to receive credit for their contribution to my reports and projects."

As mentioned in the chapter on dealing with difficult supervisors, the boss's failure to give them credit is a pet peeve of subordinates. It certainly can't hurt you if you give your staff credit for doing part of a report or project, can it? If you don't, you'll probably have de-motivated them for the next report or project they're involved with. The main goal of supervisors is to motivate staff to do their best work. Doesn't it make sense to give them credit for good work?

Job descriptions

"My staff expects me to change job descriptions to suit their own talents and abilities!"

Many progressive-thinking firms are doing just that. Instead of pushing employees to fit the needs of the company, many are adapting positions to match the employee's talents and abilities. Until all firms do this, employees must conform to the needs of the position they're hired to fill.

"I don't fully believe in job descriptions because they just encourage staff to state, 'That's not in my job description.'"

As discussed earlier, accurate, up-to-date job descriptions are essential for an employee to do good work. How can your staff possibly do a good job for you and your company if they don't know exactly what's expected from them? Clearly define each task, giving standards of performance (quality, quantity, time and occasionally cost) for each one. Then, and only then, will both you and your staff know what's expected of them.

Lack of training funds

"My training budget is nil, but my staff want and expect training."

It's not a nice place for a supervisor to be, but it happens in bad economic times. It's not always possible for companies to provide all the funds for training, but there can usually be some compromises. Some companies have employees sign a document stating that employees will have to reimburse their company for the cost of training, if they leave the company within two years of training. Alternatively, the company could pay for half the training costs.

If employees require training, the supervisor must show management the cost-effectiveness of the training. Itemise the ways in which the training will benefit the company. Try to identify the financial benefits to the company. If the company still proves ungenerous, encourage staff to pay for the training themselves. Explain the benefits to them of additional future salary as compared to the cost of training - that it's an investment in their future.

Performance Appraisals

"My staff want regular performance appraisals, but my company doesn't give them."

It's a common practice in most businesses to have at least a yearly performance appraisal for each employee. As well, appraisals are often conducted at the end of the employee's probationary period. They're highly recommended, to make employees aware of how they're doing. Some firms offer performance appraisals after each special project.

There are many kinds of performance appraisals. Most are extremely poor because they evaluate subjective things such as attitude, judgment and initiative. This type of evaluation depends heavily on the mood of the person preparing the appraisal.

Instead, employees should be evaluated on whether they reached planned objectives. Each objective would include standards of performance. This method takes the uncertainty out of performance appraisals. Both the employee and the supervisor know exactly how the employee is doing because the evaluation is based on facts rather than on the supervisor's personal impressions.

If your company doesn't conduct regular performance appraisals, suggest it start to do so. State that you intend to have such appraisals for your own staff, even if the company doesn't. In many cases, when one department initiates an appraisal system, employees in other departments soon see the benefits and lobby for the system to be used throughout the company. Try it - you've got nothing to lose.

Proper wages for work done

"My company doesn't have a personnel department. How do I choose proper salary ranges for my staff?"

Call your competitors and find what they pay people with skills and abilities like those of your staff. Watch newspaper advertisements describing positions like those in your company. Don't be cheap – it's better to overpay slightly than to underpay and lose good employees.

Sacking older employees

"Should I follow the trend of replacing older, more expensive staff with younger, less expensive staff?"

This is a tough question to answer. It's often the only answer some companies see to solve economic problems. A more junior person at $50,000 a year could replace a senior, long-term employee who may be five years away from retirement and earns $90,000.

Many companies have been offering their senior staff early retirement as a humane compromise. Some firms, however, simply decide to make their senior, more expensive staff redundant. Not only is this usually devastating for the employee, but other staff soon begin to wonder when their turn will come. Employees the company may wish to keep may seek other jobs and leave at inconvenient times. Morale may suffer and affect productivity adversely.

Although there aren't any easy answers to this problem, companies need to consider the pros and cons very carefully before deciding to follow this trend.

Motivating aggressive staff

Real tests of a supervisor's skill are employees who appear to be poorly motivated but have the potential to be great assets to the company. Such employees often have a great deal of energy that shows itself in negative, aggressive, even trouble-making behaviour. This negative behaviour could be caused by:

- The feeling that they lack job security;
- The feeling that they lack the necessary education, experience or knowledge;
- Lack of self-esteem or pride in their own skills, abilities and achievements;
- Work that under-uses their skills and abilities;
- The feeling of not fitting in with their work group (perhaps because of racial and/or cultural differences).

Those who believe they don't fit into their positions for whatever reason, may act aggressively towards their company, top management, supervisors, co-workers or clients. Supervisors seeking to *"turn around"* employees of this type could:

- Give authentic compliments on the work completed;
- Explain to the employees how valuable their efforts are to their fellow workers (part of the team);
- Explain the importance of their jobs to the company;
- Show that their training and other qualifications equip them to do more than just a satisfactory job;
- Provide some measure of recognition for their work accomplishments;
- Bring them into group situations; ask for their advice;
- Carefully describe the responsibilities of their position and set *reachable* performance standards.

Many aggressive employees have a great deal to offer. They may be very success-oriented and willing to accept challenges and to set high standards for themselves to achieve recognition. Their energy level is often high, so that supervisors may find it difficult to keep them constructively occupied. Power also stimulates these people, and they may respond well if given some authority as soon as they're able to handle it. Delegate responsibilities that allow them to take charge but watch carefully for abuse of other co-workers or clients. These employees may be poor delegators and unwilling to ask for the help that they need. They may prefer to work alone. Give them that chance if possible. Such employees also tend to enjoy variety, so try to change their tasks often.

Staff who are resisting change

When supervisors want to make changes in the methods their subordinates use to complete assignments, the resistance they meet often surprises them. This is especially true right now with so many technological changes happening.

Do you have trouble adjusting to change? Can you think of a situation that's facing you now that involves change? If you're able to identify one, ask yourself, *"What can go wrong if I refuse to change?"* Then decide what the advantages will be of changing now, rather than later, when you'll have no choice.

Supervisors and trainers need to be aware of the stages people go through when adjusting to change to help them make the transition as smoothly as possible. These four stages are:

1. *Unfreezing:* During this initial stage you require employees to give up their regular way of doing things and identify new methods. This involves breaking old habits.

2. *Changing:* The new pattern of behaviour, or new way of doing something is explained and taught. Before this can be done the supervisor needs to identify the advantages of the change and the reasons why it might provoke resistance. Ways of overcoming objections to the change should also be identified

3. *Refreezing:* Employees' use of the new method is monitored until it takes hold. Supervisors must catch die-

hards who are determined to do it the old way. This can take up to three months of constant surveillance.

4. **Commitment:** People are ready to make plans that utilize the new way.

Overcoming objections to change

New systems, methods and designs won't work unless you get people to accept new ideas. You might have to sell your ideas. This is where planning comes in. For example, suppose you've found a faster way of processing clients' orders. Before explaining the new system to others, prepare by:

a. Writing a summary of the existing method;

b. Determining the advantages and disadvantages of this method;

c. Writing a summary of the new method;

d. Determining the advantages and disadvantages of the new method;

e. Anticipating the objections others will raise and deciding what you will say to defend your new idea.

The following checklist will help you cope with objections from others more effectively.

- Anticipate and prepare for as many possible objections as you can. Develop a plan for handling each of them.

- Ask staff to explain their objections in very specific terms with examples.

- Don't be content with superficial reasons for resistance to a change. Dig until you discover the real reasons.

- Work out a practical way of overcoming each objection if you possibly can.

- If you're unable to overcome an objection, try to find a way to compensate for it.

- Rally enough benefits to win the person's support and cooperation despite the objection.

- Find a way to ease the person's mind, to make it less risky to go along with you despite the objection.

- With habitual or chronic objectors, introduce your idea gradually. Don't try to get immediate acceptance or compliance. The objection may be nothing more than a delaying tactic – the person's natural resistance to change.

- Consider bringing up significant objections yourself instead of waiting for others to do so. Then explain how these can be overcome.

Correcting or Disciplining Staff

These are responses that show acceptance and understanding of the feelings of the person you're talking with and acknowledge his or her efforts to grow and change.

1. *"Do you feel you're not getting cooperation from...?"*

2. *"How can I help you get this roadblock removed?"*

3. *"You believe you have the skills to complete this task?"*

Exploratory questions

These are responses made to encourage further examination, even though the facts may be unpleasant.

1. *"Tell me more about that."*

2. *"What seems to be the difficulty here?"*

3. *"When did this first start?"*

4. *"How does this relate to your performance?"*

"I never know how to start a performance appraisal interview where I have to correct someone's behaviour. Should I start by telling the person all their good qualities and attributes, before I concentrate on the ones I want changed?"

Start by giving a brief overall summary of the employee's behaviour (trying to emphasise the good-news aspect), then discuss the behaviour you want to correct, and end by refocusing on the employee's strengths.

Think back to conversations you've had with former bosses. Did you hear one word they said while they were expressing their views on what you did right? Probably you didn't. We seem to wait for that special word *"but,"* and we seldom hear anything that precedes it. Most people do things right about 95 per cent of the time but feel hurt about the 5 per cent that requires correction.

Because of this, you should start by talking about the 5 per cent they've done wrong. Explain that the important thing is that they learn from their mistakes and don't make them again. Then you can use the rest of the interview to tell them what they've done right. This concludes the meeting with positive feelings and results in a more pleasant ending for both of you. The employee knows what needs to be corrected but isn't left with a feeling of failure.

CHAPTER ELEVEN
DEALING WITH UNPRODUCTIVE BEHAVIOUR

The term *"unproductive behaviour"* covers a multitude of items, from intractable inefficiency to theft. To correct some of these you need little more than well-honed communication skills. Others may require you to exercise all the supervisory and managerial skills at your command.

Buck-passing Employees

In today's complex managerial environment, it's becoming increasing important to avoid even minor errors. Buck-passing can be a symptom of a supervisor's failure to delegate responsibility correctly or to define responsibilities clearly. Formal policy-and-procedures manuals that define responsibility would eliminate some of this buck-passing.

It's not enough for supervisors to tell employees how to do their jobs. They must also explain exactly what their responsibilities are. For example, *"Wilma, you're responsible for correctly matching freight bills to the duplicate of the receiving report."*

"What if there are differences?"

"It's part of your duty to note the differences on the voucher to Accounts Payable. Any mistakes in matching will be your fault. Any questions?"

Even a well-qualified employee like Wilma will make mistakes. However, she'll make fewer and fewer mistakes and won't attempt to pass the buck if you keep reminding her of the responsibilities of her position.

Try not to over-discipline for any errors. Too heavy a disciplinary hand only invites excuses (e.g. *"The dispatcher said it's okay to approve trucking bills, so I thought this was okay too."* Or, *"Don't blame me for that one! John said it was okay to approve it"*).

Overly severe disciplinary action for mistakes has other adverse effects besides buck-passing. It causes lying, cheating and hiding of mistakes. The concealment of mistakes causes irreparable harm to the company. Service failures can be expensive. The cost of the immediate replacement of the service plus the lowered image of the company results in decreases in sales or service volume.

From time to time, supervisors should set an example by admitting to mistakes themselves in the presence of their subordinates. This can demonstrate to others that passing the buck is not acceptable.

Bottleneck Employees

"The work isn't getting out because John's sitting on it!" Bottlenecks are a frequent management complaint. A bottleneck is someone or something that stops the flow of work. It often results in employees' inactivity while they wait for the bottleneck to clear. The causes could be attributable to either the design of the workflow or the employee's personal work habits. If you suspect poor design of the workflow, try this simple test. Have another employee assume the duties of the employee in the problem area. If there's still a bottleneck (after a period of training), make changes in the work flow arrangement.

Bottleneck employees are typically characterized by:

- Tendency to be derailed by relatively minor problems;
- Not enough training;
- Low decision-making capability;
- Ignorance of productivity requirements.
- Lack of team-member identity;
- Job insecurity;
- Unusual fear of making mistakes;
- Incompatibility with co-workers leading to lack of cooperation.

If there's no indication that the bottleneck is deliberately caused, perhaps the bottleneck employee is not clear about what you want. The supervisor should reinforce the employee's training. During this retraining, the supervisor can see if the employee comprehends the job in detail, demonstrate to the employee how to perform the various tasks and then guide the employee under direct observation. The emphasis should be on techniques that can speed up completion of the job.

Employees should know how their job fits in with others in the company. They then have knowledge of the consequences of their own good or bad performance.

Most stick-in-the-mud employees don't really want to be that way. Most want to feel that they are cooperating in achieving common goals. The secret to dealing with this is to make everyone in the workforce have a common goal. Supervisors should enlist the help of the other employees by saying: *"Tom, can you show Richard how we can move that project faster?"*

"Richard, let Tom show you a couple of techniques for pushing the stuff through that we need now."

An important element in removing the bottleneck is to make the problem employee want to put the work out faster. The paying of a few compliments here and there improves confidence among slower employees. It permits them to have a greater feeling of job security and certainly reduces tensions. The bottleneck employee who feels more in control will have less fear of making mistakes. In short, some additional coaching, coupled with a reduction in tension, may free the employee to move faster.

Error-Prone Employees

There are two basic kinds of accidents. One type results from systems design. The methods or techniques used permit a certain number of errors. Constant improvement of the system reduces the error rate. However, no matter how well the system is designed, the human factor must be considered as well.

The following conditions may be at fault:

- Inadequate job training;
- Limited written instructions;
- Too many subordinates reporting to one supervisor;
- Too few intermediate levels of supervision;
- Dull work environment;
- Employees bored with their jobs;
- No studies done to determine error causes;
- High employee-turnover rate.

Car insurance companies recognize that some drivers are more prone to having accidents than the general population of drivers. Some employees are more likely to make mistakes than others. Deliberate mistakes should result in disciplinary actions, up to and including firing of the employee. However, most mistakes aren't intentional. They're caused by a variety of factors including errors in judgment on the part of management or lack of employee training. Suggested steps to reduce errors are:

1. Determine the nature of errors.
2. Revise the system to improve error detection.
3. Use a senior employee as a coach to an error-prone employee.
4. Appeal to the employee's pride of workmanship.
5. Have a chat with an error-prone employee to review causes of mistakes.

Most employees like to feel that they're earning their pay. Part of that feeling of pride stems from their opinion that their work has few, if any, errors. Therefore, they appreciate help, when it is offered gracefully, in improving their own pride in their work. One method of attack is to provide an employee coach for the error-prone employee.

Senior employees who are proficient in their work can help isolate the *causes* of their problem employee's errors. Rather than catching mistakes *after* the fact and taking corrective action, they can provide instruction to help avoid errors. The problem employee may simply need to be told which points require additional attention (e.g., *"Bryan, can you spend a little more effort on re-checking?"* Or, *"Marcia, can you pay a little more attention to these types of items?"*).

To reinforce pride of workmanship, don't let employees describe their positions as *"just a janitor"* or *"just a receptionist."* Be ready to explain their importance to the smooth running of your company.

Daydreamers

We all daydream, but some people do it to excess – to a point where it results in low productivity, errors and accidents. Some jobs lend themselves more to employee daydreaming than others and need more thorough monitoring.

It's not always fair to pin the blame for daydreaming on the employees themselves. Their jobs may be so boring that they can't keep their minds on the task. Robotic-like duties invite employee daydreaming.

Work that requires employee creativity should have an environment that's conducive to creativity. Where different and varied types of work proceed through a section, it's advisable to use job rotation to alleviate monotony. Adding flexibility in the method of performing the job will allow the employees to decide how to handle individual steps. Such flexibility permits employees to think about how they want to complete tasks. This, in turn, increases alertness and reduces monotony. The use of job rotation provides some cross training (more people know different jobs). This gives supervisors a greater flexibility in the use of their staff and provides more than one worker who is qualified to fill the position.

Jobs should be designed to hold the employee's attention. Tasks performed while the person is standing discourage daydreaming. Better design of the work area can also help. The décor of the work area is of some importance. Desks or work areas need not be the same colour. Make every effort to remove monotony in the work environment. Recommended steps are:

1. Evaluate the environment. Make any changes possible.

2. Revise workflow to reduce monotony.

3. Develop alternative methods and order of steps to accomplish the work.

4. Where possible, let the employee decide what s/he is to produce that day.

5. Identify employees who require constant supervisor prompting to improve attentiveness.

No matter what efforts you make to dispel daydreaming, some employees remain lost in the clouds. Only constant supervisory attention can dispel the problem and keep the employee on his or her toes. In this case, a discussion between the supervisor and the employee is in order. It may become necessary to replace the worker.

Messy work station

Many consider good housekeeping as window dressing. They explain *"I know where everything is on my desk."* It's when they're away because of illness that their messiness causes difficulties. Others who take over can't find things. In fact, poor housekeepers often *don't* know where everything is, and an unduly messy work area may be a sign of inefficiency. Excessive untidiness can result in:

- Missing records or files;
- Lost or misplaced tools or equipment;
- High supply costs;
- An improper mix of parts and inventory;
- Contamination of the product;
- High scrap and reworking costs;
- A poor balance of finished products in inventory;
- High machine downtime;

- A poor safety record;
- Low employee morale and reluctance to work overtime;
- Discipline problems and labour turnover.

Motivate your employees to maintain a tidy work area by your example. Good housekeeping habits are more easily encouraged among your staff if your own office is kept neat and clean. Encourage clean-ups at the end of each day. If you spot employees whose workstations look messy heading for the door, stop them. Ask them to organise their workstation before leaving. You may have to provide a written checklist of housekeeping activities they are to follow.

Dishonest Employees

There was a time when thefts from inventory affected only industries that had attractive types of inventory. Increasingly, however, all types of inventory are becoming subject to theft. Not only completed assemblies, but also parts and even raw materials are being stolen.

Employees who take home a few coloured pencils for their children may not cost the company much, but they set a bad attitudinal example. Some employees go far beyond a few pencils. Theft is often a way of *"getting back at management"*. Some of these people who steal far more than they could ever use. Usually, employees who constantly steal are unsatisfactory employees, not only because of their thieving, but for other reasons as well. It's not just that they have low regard for company property, but they think little of the company that employs them.

It's not economically justifiable to lock everything up, nor is it possible to catch all the culprits. However, if management removes some of the temptations, they'll have fewer losses. Having only one or two people in charge of the company office supplies is one way of cutting down on pilfering. Having employees sign for stationery and equipment is another.

Time wasters

Personal Telephone Calls

Nothing's as annoying to a supervisor as watching an employee receive an excessive number of personal telephone calls. It's not just that the lines are being tied up; the flow of work is also interrupted. If employees waste company time, they waste the company money allotted for their salaries. Employees should keep personal calls to a minimum. After all, they are at a place of business, and personal-life requirements should wait until after work.

Employees who conduct personal business on company time are often overlooked for promotions. Most don't even understand what they've done to hamper their progress in the company.

Strategies to alleviate this problem include:

1. Telling employees to limit personal phone calls to important or emergency calls, which should be kept short and sweet. Have them advise their friends and relatives about the company policy. No more than one or two personal calls a day should be necessary.

2. Requiring the switchboard operator to ask an incoming caller for his or her name and to say, *"What company do you represent?"* That question alone may be enough to reduce non-business calls and their duration. The switchboard operator might keep track of non-business calls for one or two days and submit a report to the supervisor of each section. Interviews with errant employees can then be arranged to reinforce the policy.

3. Many companies now have voice mail with direct numbers. It is harder for companies to monitor this situation. Regular reinforcement by management about personal calls may be necessary to remind employees about the company's policies.

4. Making sure employees realise that their behaviour may be keeping them from being promoted to a higher position.

Coffee and Lunch Break Abuse

Studies show that breaks in the work schedule increase production. At the same time, supervisors need to guard against the tendency of employees to slow down in anticipation of coffee or lunch breaks. Many employees will extend their breaks if there is no pressure on them not to do so. After the break, work should begin right away. If you've identified this as a problem, be visible immediately before and after breaks. This enables you to observe abuses directly and to encourage more productive use of your employee's time. After the break, you could hand out assignments or check employees' progress.

Only a conscientious effort on the part of supervisory personnel will segregate those who occasionally abuse breaks from those who consistently do so. Despite supervisory efforts, some employees will continue to abuse coffee and lunch breaks. This warrants formal disciplinary action (written warning on file, suspension for the day, etc.).

Absenteeism

Many employees will go to work even with a runny nose and a fever. They refuse to take advantage of their company's sick-pay policy. Many feel they don't wish to take sick leave for minor ailments because they may need the leave when they're really sick. Others feel that no one else can handle their job as well as they can. They feel responsible for their performance. To them, it's part of the ethic of being a good worker. The supervisor should recognise the sacrifices made by this kind of worker. When that type of employee is out ill, s/he is usually too sick to perform any kind of work at all. Such employees are assets to any company. Unfortunately, however, most companies also have their share of employees who abuse their sick-leave privileges. In fact, in any normal working day, usually from 4 to 6 per cent of all employees are absent from work.

Absenteeism disrupts the flow of work and causes delays and production problems. The quality of work suffers because employees replaced by others are not as well trained or because overtime is needed to complete the extra work.

Because the costs to the company of abuses of sick leave are high, all supervisors need to take steps to discourage unwarranted absenteeism.

Such steps include:

Enforcing the rules. Otherwise employees will keep on abusing them, and others may be encouraged to do so as well;

Determining if there are absenteeism patterns. The five major types of unwarranted absenteeism are listed below along with some strategies for dealing with them. (Note: some solutions may not be compatible with your company's union agreements. Make sure you're aware of these before acting.)

Chronic absenteeism

Chronic absentees are often negative thinkers. Everyday frustrations and pressures easily overwhelm them. They consistently have unwarranted absences that usually follow a pattern. This type of employee calls and says, *"Sorry boss, but I can't make it in today."* You may be tempted to reply, *"I'm sorry you're sick. Stay away until you're feeling better."* However, don't say that. Don't worry. These employees will stay away until they feel a lot better, with or without your blessing. They view their sick leave as a right.

How many times a year do employees pull that line before you consider them chronic absentees? One company identifies problem employees by eight absences a year, or more than one or more days each month in a year.

For those suspected of abusing their sick-leave privileges, the supervisor should call the employee at the end of each working day and say, *"Orson, how are you coming along? I'm calling to see if you expect to be back to work tomorrow."*

Using this tactic allows two beautiful spin-off benefits to happen. First, you've determined that the absent employee is really at home. Of course, s/he could have been at the doctor's

- but not *every* time you called. Second, you will discourage the employee from taking sick leave for minor ailments or to accomplish personal chores.

When the employee returns to work, the supervisor should:

- State, *"Sure missed you yesterday. We really need and depend on you"*:

- Describe the problems the employee's absence caused the department;

- Encourage the employee to be in more often;

- Explain the consequences if similar instances occur too often.

- Insist on a medical certificate from their doctor.

Innocent Absenteeism

Innocent absenteeism, even if it's excessive, doesn't warrant disciplinary action. On the other hand, an employee's inability to report regularly for work, *for whatever reasons,* provides grounds for termination of employment. In such cases:

1. The employer must be able to document the employee's absences. These absences must be well beyond what any reasonable person would consider acceptable. The employee must have deviated substantially and unduly from the average level of attendance of other employees.

2. The employer must be able to demonstrate that the excessive-absenteeism problem has been persistent. It must have continued despite *documented* attempts by the employer to have it corrected. The supervisor must keep a record of his or her efforts to counsel the employee and to determine the underlying reasons for absences. The supervisor must be able to show that s/he has been compassionate and has taken extenuating circumstances into account.

3. The employer must be able to present convincing reasons explaining why s/he feels there's little or no likelihood of improvement.

An employee who falsifies a doctor's certificate should receive a written warning, which is placed on his or her file, or possibly termination. The degree of discipline depends on the circumstances in each situation.

If an employee is absent for more than three days in a row without calling in, it can be assumed that s/he has abandoned the job. This could result in dismissal.

When an employee's excessive absenteeism is due to a drinking problem, the employer may discharge the employee. The employer must be able to demonstrate that the employment relationship cannot continue. The company must be able to defend its decision and show that it has recognized the alcoholic problem as an illness, and it must be able to prove that it has made an honest effort to help the employee correct the illness.

Goof-Off absenteeism

These absentees typically decide to enjoy themselves (go golfing perhaps) rather than do what they consider dull, repetitious work that they believe wastes their abilities. They feel the need to escape the humdrum environment of work. This can lock them into a vicious circle, because these people are seldom considered for the promotions, they think they need and deserve. To help them lose this need to escape, the supervisor should:

1. Confront them with their absenteeism record.

2. Ask why it's happening.

3. Encourage them to use their sick leave properly. Explain that **sick leave is a privilege; not a right** and should be used only for *their own* authentic illnesses, *not for personal reasons or for their children's or spouse's illnesses* (unless special leave for these reasons is allowed by the company).

4. Make sure that they are aware that their absence record is a major factor keeping them from being promoted.

5. Identify rewards (e.g., a promotion) that may be obtained with good attendance. This is far better than using

punishment (written warnings on file) to bring about changes in behaviour.

Naïve absenteeism

Many employees believe that management expects and condones phoney absences. These employees also believe that if they have sick leave coming, they have a right to take it whenever they please. Employee morale breaks down when employees get away with calling in sick and get paid for the day, when they weren't sick at all. While it's difficult to determine with complete certainty who is truly ill and who isn't, supervisors should make sure that employees don't abuse sick leave. To deal with this, supervisors should:

- Confront employees regarding their absenteeism record;

- Explain what sick leave is for (a privilege, not a right). Tell them that they're doing important work and that the company suffers when they're away;

- Encourage employees to use absences properly - for legitimate illness;

- Ask employees to identify what effects their absence has had on other employees.

Abusive Absenteeism

Some employees will be away for any and every minor ailment. They demonstrate little sense of responsibility for any required productivity. It is of little concern to them if their absence means that other workers need to carry a larger workload or that their company will suffer economically. These employees are usually unhappy, feel victimised and believe that others receive favouritism. They break company rules and have many conflicts with their supervisors. They pick fights and believe that they're always right and others are always wrong. If you must deal with such employees:

- Be direct about the penalties for continuing the abuse. *"Your job is on the line unless you conform to the rules of this company."* Tell them you'll have to replace them if their record doesn't improve, that they must produce doctors' reports for absenteeism, etc. Stick to the facts and be firm and clear about the consequences;

- Compliment them on the work they do when they are conforming to the rules.

Legitimate absenteeism

Authentic illnesses, bereavement, jury duty and necessary personal business, such as dentist and doctor's appointments are legitimate reasons for taking time off. However, employers shouldn't pay sick leave to those who take time off for their children's illnesses (this should be time off without pay, unless company policy states otherwise).

Absenteeism Policies

When industries rely on individual performance, any absence is a disruption in the flow of service to customers. To help reduce absenteeism, many companies have implemented stiffer proof-of-illness procedures. They may:

- Require a doctor's certificate for any absence of three or more sick days a week;

- Require a doctor's certificate for *any* absence due to illness, or after a holiday weekend;

- Require a complete physical examination by the company doctor if the employee is away for more than ten days in any one year.

Dealing with Personality Clashes

When two of your staff have a personality clash, how and when should you intervene?

If two employees don't get along, the one who suffers most is their supervisor. You may find that Bob and George are excellent workers but harass each other and fail to cooperate. If the conflict arises from work-related cause and affects their productivity or that of others, the supervisor will have to help the employees resolve their disagreement. Frequently though, the cause is something related to the basic nature of the two personalities involved. Even the cleverest supervisors will find it impossible to change people's personalities. The most they can hope to do is to get the two employees to work reasonably well together despite their admitted personality differences.

One recommended method is to call both parties into a private office. Let both, in turn, state what they think the problems are and blow off a little steam. Then act as an impartial mediator whose only interest is to keep up production. *You must let these employees know that you will not tolerate the situation as it is.*

Encourage the employees to discuss ways of resolving the problem and to agree on a course of corrective action. Keep a close watch on the situation and call further interviews if warranted. Make sure both employees know what the consequences will be if their negative behaviour continues.

Dealing with Emotional People

If we've caused a person to feel badly and s/he reacts emotionally, we normally comfort that person - and rightly so. In the work place, however, you need to keep your distance from employees who become emotional. For example, you may be a supervisor who has the unpleasant tasks of disciplining, dismissing or laying off an employee. Perhaps the person is in tears and very embarrassed about it. How can you make this situation easier for both people?

One of my tasks when I worked in human resources was the chore of laying off or firing employees. Because I'm a real softy, I would occasionally become emotional along with the person being laid off or disciplined. By accident, I found a way of helping both of us regain our equilibrium.

I achieved this when I handed the person a box of tissues and said, *"I have something I need to attend to. I'll be back in a few minutes."* I then left the room and took a few deep breaths. When I felt I had my emotions under control, I went back to my office.

Because I had given the person the same opportunity to calm down, she had regained her composure and some of her self-respect. We were able to continue the conversation until we took care of all the issues.

Save using this tactic for situations that warrant it. Many people use tears to get sympathy and will try to manipulate you with their tears. When dealing with this type, I gave them a box of tissues and continued the conversation.

Dealing with Racial and Ethnic Slurs

Most work places, if they're in compliance with the law, are a mixture of individuals of different backgrounds. Companies show poor management if they ignore or tolerate a racial or ethnic slur against an employee, a supervisor, a customer or a member of the public. Such derogatory language is bad public relations for the company and causes problems between employees.

Jokes at the expense of someone else, aren't jokes at all. Managers should never knowingly joke about someone's background or personal appearance or condone such behaviour in their employees. One can't judge on the surface how such a joke might affect an individual. Racial or ethnic slurs stem from prejudice. Prejudice is based on stereotypical views and generalizations about a group and shows a lack of respect for people as individuals.

Supervisors should clearly demonstrate management's attitude towards prejudice by openly showing their disapproval of any racial or ethnic slur. The supervisor may also need to interview the offender privately. The person may insist that his or her comments are harmless. The supervisor's reply should be, *"Charlie, they may be* meant *to be harmless, but they have a harmful effect, so keep your thoughts to yourself."*

If the problem continues, the supervisor should say, *"Charlie, performance appraisals show how employees get along with the other employees and customers. I wouldn't like to place a comment on your file that you don't get along. However, if you continue to make these disparaging remarks, I'll have to place a written warning on your file. Do you understand?"*

Prejudice against Female Supervisors

Anti-female prejudice can be found in both men and women who believe that men are superior to women and that the world should be male dominated. This is one of the most serious problems women still face in the work place today. How should women respond to such prejudice?

Some anti-female attitudes are openly expressed so that you're in no doubt that the person is out to keep women in their *"place"*. However, many people aren't aware that their attitude could be considered biased. These are often older men, or men whose upbringing or home situation kept women in traditionally subservient positions. Many of these men call women *"dear"* because women are dear to them. Such men protect women; they feel it's their duty to do so. This type of man doesn't mean to harm women and usually doesn't understand why women are offended by certain remarks. In these cases, a gentle response is necessary. Use of the feedback technique will give these men the opportunity to change their behaviour.

Many men still call women *"girls"* which they haven't been since entering their teens. This also offends some women.

Many older women also suffer from an anti-female bias. They have been conditioned to believe women should be subservient and think of women who compete with others, supervise men or hold positions of power as un-feminine. They look down on such women, especially if they aren't married or have no intention of having children.

Anti-female attitudes are not uncommon in younger and middle-aged women. For instance, women who won't accept orders from female supervisors unconsciously feel that only men should be supervisors. They question the ability of their female supervisors and make things difficult for them.

Support staff (who are still mainly women) normally go out of their way to keep their supervisors and managers (who are still usually male) organised, on time and comfortable. They nurture their supervisors (bring them coffee, remind them of appointments, open their mail). The nurturing may stop when a woman is appointed to a supervisory position, unless she's on top of things. She sometimes needs to let her staff know that she expects the same kind of help that the former male supervisor received.

Older Subordinates

Janet had a problem that at one time was rare but is quite common now. By the time she was twenty-five, she held the position of clerical supervisor. Her college education had prepared her for the position, and she had four years' experience in an office. However, she found herself unprepared to supervise women in the office almost twice her age. These women had an average of ten to fifteen years' office experience. They were openly hostile to her and quite uncooperative.

Janet decided to talk to Sarah, one of the less-hostile older women, to discuss the problem. Sarah was honest. She admitted she had been surprised and disappointed when Janet had been *"hired off the street"* as her supervisor. She had pictured someone her own age or older filling the position - possibly one of her peer group or someone whose experience she felt would give her the *"right"* to supervise. Instead, she found a woman the same age as her daughter in the role.

She admitted that when Janet complimented her on a job well done, she felt patronised, and when she was criticised, she felt defensive. Once these feelings were brought out into the open, the two women were able to start over. Janet now understood the reasons for Sarah's antagonism and could deal with it better. Sarah had clarified why she felt as she did and tried to change her attitude towards Janet.

Soon after, Janet called a meeting with the rest of her staff to discuss the situation with them. She said that she understood how they felt and explained to them what she expected from each of them. She then added that she was relying on them to cooperate and asked each staff member, *"Can I count on you in the future?"* One of her employees, Julie, appeared reluctant to make such a commitment, so Janet knew she would have to keep an eye on her. Soon the woman's low productivity and negative attitude made it necessary for Janet to discipline her. She again explained to Julie what she expected from her and what the consequences would be if Julie kept on producing sloppy work. Unfortunately, Julie never did accept Janet. She kept on producing sloppy work and eventually had to be fired.

Janet fared better with the others. When she noticed a decided change in attitude and productivity, she thanked them for their understanding and cooperation.

Traditionally, society has taught us that the older woman (the mother or aunt) knows more, so therefore should be treated with respect. These feelings revolve around power, and who should rightly have it. There is no cut-and-dried solution to the problem.

Male Subordinates

Barbara supervised a staff of three men. She was an engineer and the men were technologists. She found that her subordinates didn't seem to listen to her and insisted on doing things their way. Fortunately, before taking the position, she had made sure that she had received proper supervisory training. This boosted her self-confidence.

Barbara found it necessary to conduct a disciplinary interview when one of her male subordinates refused to do a task assigned to him. This was a case of insubordination (a very serious infraction) that could have led to the dismissal of the employee. She handled it herself and placed a strong written warning on the employee's file, stating that he would be fired if his negative behaviour continued. She made sure her manager was aware of her actions, and he commended her on the competent way she had handled the touchy situation.

Aggressive Female Label

Her subordinates and co-workers had labelled Margaret, a supervisor, *"aggressive"*. She felt that she was just doing her job the way she had seen other supervisors do it.

She had copied her male counterparts' behaviour and language. It didn't work in her case and she had been labelled an *"aggressive female."*

Her appearance and body language suggested that she was a forceful, self-assured, rather pushy individual. These qualities are readily accepted in men, but less readily in women. I explained that her tone of voice could be the problem, or possibly her forceful body language.

Questioning revealed that she tended to give instructions in the form of orders rather than requests - *"You will..."*, rather than, *"I'd like you to...."* She agreed to tone down her speech and body language. It worked.

Other supervisory problems

Passing on difficult clients

"My front-line people are always referring their difficult clients to me instead of handling them themselves."

Help them acquire the skills they need to deal with these difficult people (give them a copy of this book, perhaps). Explain to them how you expect them to deal with abusive, profane or threatening behaviour. You may instruct them to hang up or transfer the caller to you.

Often irate clients take all their irritability out on clerical staff and are as sweet as pie with supervisors or managers. Don't assume that your clerical staff were exaggerating about the unpleasant behaviour of the client. Identify what is and is not acceptable client behaviour. Support your staff when they've been mistreated. Explain to the client, *"We don't tolerate harassment of our staff. I suggest you apologize to Margie about the way you spoke to her."*

Want me to "bend the rules"

"Top management says we can bend the rules for special clients. My staff objects."

I don't blame them. Nothing is as annoying as saying *"No"* to clients who then go over your head and persuade some higher up to say *"Yes."* Support your staff by discussing the situation with your manager. Ask management for some hard and fast rules. Explain the difficulties that have resulted. Give concrete examples, demonstrating the costs in hard feelings, poor morale, etc. The better you're prepared before you confront management, the less chance there will be that they will turn you down. If management does turn down your request, explain what has happened to your staff.

Enforcing rules and regulations

"How can I help my staff feel comfortable when they have to enforce unpopular rules and regulations?"

Teach them the stuck-record technique. Request that they use this technique without raising their voices or showing annoyance of any kind. Help them develop the necessary responses, such as, *"I'm sorry. I'd like to make an exception in your case, but I can't bend the rules for anyone."* Instruct them to repeat the relevant form of words as often as necessary. Be ready to back them up if someone attempts to go over their head.

Must cut staff

"How can I handle having to cut staff, which makes four people do the work of five?"

This becomes necessary when the economy forces companies to *"tighten their belts."* If you haven't taken a time management course; now's the time to do so. It will teach you how to set priorities and concentrate on the most important tasks. In doing so you will set a good example for your staff. If you help your subordinates to use good time management techniques, you may find that four people *can* do the work of five and do so effectively.

Learn to cut corners and try new methods for completion of tasks. Have meetings with your staff to discuss easier, quicker ways of doing tasks. Listen to their ideas carefully. Because they're the ones who are doing the tasks, they often come up with the best timesaving suggestions.

Misinterpretation of instructions

"My staff is always misinterpreting my instructions."

Use the paraphrasing technique to check that they have understood what you want. This technique is most effective when you're giving instructions or training someone. It will confirm to you that they heard what you said. Be careful when asking for paraphrasing that you don't make it sound as if you think they're too stupid to understand your instructions. It is your responsibility to be sure your instructions are clear, not theirs to interpret a confusing message. Put complex information on paper.

Staff wasting my time

"My staff want me to spend my valuable time answering their unimportant questions."

Many supervisors may get angry at interruptions, but many others inadvertently encourage helplessness in their subordinates. When an employee comes to them with a problem, some supervisors immediately provide the solution. It would be better if they first asked, *"What do you think you should do about this?"* It's surprising how often the employee *does* know what to do. This strategy encourages independent thinking by employees. When they realise that they often have the answers already, and that you support them, they'll have more faith in their own judgment in the future.

If subordinates really don't know the answer, help them. That's what you're there for.

Disciplining my staff

"I hate disciplining my staff!"

It's possible that you weren't trained properly for your supervisory position. Get this training so you'll feel more comfortable when giving discipline. Remember that everything your subordinates do makes *you* look good or bad. If you allow them to do careless work, you'll be setting yourself up for a reprimand yourself. The aim of discipline is to correct poor productivity or behaviour problems, not to instil a desire to retaliate in the employee. Discipline, done correctly, moves the guilt from the shoulders of the supervisor onto those of the person being disciplined. The employee is told what the consequences will be if the unacceptable behaviour continues. Get supervisory training - especially on how to discipline employees!

Dealing with "heel nippers"

"I'm not quite ready to retire. How do I handle the 'heel-nippers' that want my job?"

This is tough. You don't want to move to the next level, but you shouldn't try to stop those who are young and eager from progressing. Suggest to them that they try another department and go around your position. Do everything in your power to get them ready for when you're ready to retire. If this is within two years, don't worry about the people behind you. Don't hamper them from being ready for your job or you'll just have unhappy, vindictive subordinates.

If you prove to them that you're interested not only in your own welfare, but also in theirs, they'll probably be more patient. They'll feel more comfortable if they know there will be an end to their waiting. Make it clear to them what your plans are. Explain that you're going to retire in two years. If it's longer than two years, you're probably going to spend the remainder of your employment bored to tears. If this is the case, keep working towards a more senior position yourself.

Unable to accept staff's new ideas

"My staff expect me to use all their bright ideas."

Judge every new idea on its own merits. Explain your conclusions, if there is some reason why it won't work. If there's some value to the idea, explain why you can or can't use the idea at that time. Keep encouraging your staff to come up with new ideas. After all, aren't they the ones who are carrying on the activities? If you stop their ideas, you'll just be de-motivating them, which is the opposite of what you want.

Wants to do things "her way"

"I have an employee who balks and wants to do things her way."

Whenever you can do so, allow your staff to complete tasks *"their"* way. If there's no room for flexibility in how a task is completed, be clear in your instructions. Explain that your instructions will bring about the results you want. If your employee continues to argue, ask her, *"Are you refusing to do this task the way I want you to do it?"* If she says, *"Yes"* you could rightfully charge her with insubordination. Try other methods first but know that your only recourse may be to place a formal written warning on her file.

Misuse of phone

"My employee is very people-oriented but is terribly disorganized. When left unsupervised he's on the phone for hours."

Use this person to make oral presentations and to deal directly with clients. Give careful, detailed instructions on what you want from him. Make sure his job description is up to date, giving standards of performance, and timelines for completion of tasks. Explain that he should not be making personal telephone calls. Initiate discipline and explain the consequences if the phone calls continue. Also consider whether he's in the right position.

Perfectionist

"My secretary is a perfectionist in everything she does, even when it's wasting valuable time. She seems to keep herself buried in her own work, doesn't seem aware of things going on around her. Because of this, she doesn't understand how her actions affect others in the department."

Give her deadlines to meet and explain the results you expect. Send her to a time management course. If you need a draft copy of something, make sure she understands that typing errors are allowed, etc. Give her information that explains how her position fits in with others in the department. This could be by showing her a copy of the organisational chart of your section or department. Explain that when she is late with her work, it has a direct effect on others. *"Margaret, when your month-end report is late, it holds up our whole department's month-end report."*

CONCLUSION

You now have the tools that will enable you to communicate more effectively with those you meet in the workplace, namely, clients, supervisors, co-workers and subordinates. These essential people skills will help you to handle all types of individuals and situations. Learn these skills, and you can't help but improve your relationships. Because these skills are now so important to business, this can lead to better assignments, promotions, more responsibility and overall improvement in employee morale.

Your people skills will help you to control your moods and keep cool under fire. Instead of becoming defensive when dealing with an irate customer, you'll concentrate on solving the client's problem. In the end both of you will be winners

You'll:

- Be a more positive person and have more time to do what *you* want to do instead of scurrying around trying to placate others;

- Be able to deal with angry or aggressive clients;

- Have the skills to deal with your own anger and stress;

- Be able to resist being coerced, manipulated or intimidated by the underhanded methods some people use to get their way. You'll also be able to identify and deal with the underlying problems;

- Be a skilful negotiator, adept at conflict resolution;

- Know how to interpret and use non-verbal signals;

- Be able to identify your own and others' passive, aggressive and assertive behaviour;

- Know how to say *"No"* without feeling guilty;

- Know how to use your communication skills to improve your effectiveness as a client, co-worker, employee or supervisor;

- Know how to deal with personality clashes;

- Understand the use of feedback to ensure that others are aware of how you feel about both the good and bad things they're doing;

- Know how to use paraphrasing to confirm that what you heard was really what was said;

- Obtain more praise and approval from your associates because you can now control your negative feelings.

Learn the techniques and practise them daily. They *do* work! Like any new skill, however, they need to be used consistently until they're automatic. When you've mastered them, you can look forward to being able to control how you deal with and react to others.

No longer will you allow others to decide what kind of day you have. Because you have gained this control, your self-esteem will rise. The more confidant you are, the less stress and anxiety you'll feel and the more energy and enthusiasm you can bring to all aspects of your life. If you use these skills, you'll need to be prepared for success, because success *will* inevitably follow!

You will find more techniques and ideas in my other books:

Dealing with Difficult People;

Dealing with difficult situations: at work and at home;

Dealing with difficult spouses and children;

Dealing with difficult relatives and in laws;

Dealing with domestic violence and child abuse;

Dealing with school bullying;

Dealing with workplace bullying; and

Retirement village bullies.

BIBLIOGRAPHY

Cava, Roberta – see list at the beginning of this book.

Tannen, Deborah – *He Said – She Said: Exploring the different ways men and women communicate* – Barnes & Noble, 2004.

Wood, Julia T – *Interpersonal Communication – everyday encounters* – Wadsworth, 2012.

Bovée, Courtland L. and *Thill, John V.* – *Business Communication Today* – Pearson Education, 2011.